MY GIFT

MY GIFT

From Bruce Layne

With Jack Sheehan

Jack Sheehan, Editor
Laura Brundige, Copy Editor
Patricia Barr, Designer

Cataloguing-in-Publication Data Available

Hardcover ISBN 1-932173-24-2.
Softcover ISBN 1-932173-05-6.

Stephens Press, LLC
A Stephens Media Group Company
Post Office Box 1600
Las Vegas, Nevada 89125-1600

Printed in Hong Kong

In deciding what to name this book, we discussed many ideas. There were good ones, bad ones, funny ones and sappy ones. In the end, I selected *My Gift* — but not primarily for the reasons those advising me suggested.

They told me it was perfect because I have a "gift" of relating with other people, and that essentially my memoirs are intended to be a "gift" to those who mean the most to me. I accepted the compliment of the former and agreed completely with the latter.

Still in all, I chose the title because I know inside my heart that my gift is the unwavering love and support I have received and continue to receive each and every day of my life from my beautiful wife, Sherry, my two sons, Chad and Trevor, and my entire extended family. Without their gift, *My Gift* would not exist.

I dedicate this book to Maddie and Garrett Bruce. Contained within are the lessons and stories of your grandfather's life. Please regard this book as a legacy of learning about the importance of perseverance, dedication, friendship, discipline, and education. Always stay positive through every storm and realize that the most important bonds of all are family ties.

I love you,

Pap Pap

To Sherry:

Through all our years together as husband and wife, the most important thing I have learned is that love is a whole lot more than flowers and candlelight. It is being together during those times when one or the other is short on patience and confidence.

In the clutch you are always willing to listen. We have been through a lot together, and yet we have always emerged stronger and closer than before. I have found joy and contentment in our love. You are very special. I know I may not tell you that as often as I should. When things get difficult, you lighten the load with your help and understanding. You are the balance and center of my life.

Love,
Bruce

Bruce and Sherry Layne, 1989.

Contents

Introduction

I had met Bruce Layne a couple of times through the years at social functions, and I recalled his run for Lieutenant Governor about 10 years ago, but I had never spoken to him at any length. So I thought it was odd that his name kept coming up in conversations with different people. In four or five instances, mutual friends of ours told me that Bruce was working on his memoirs, and that he needed help. One even said that Bruce was going to call me to get some advice.

But I heard nothing. And then one more person out of the blue told me that Bruce was in need of some editorial help, so I gave him a call. I was working on two other book projects at the time and didn't see how I could offer more than a few quick suggestions about different ways he might approach the challenge of writing his story. But I volunteered to meet with Bruce and see how I might assist him.

At our first meeting, in his insurance office in Henderson, I could see that many hours had already gone into his project. There were notes and outlines and questionnaires and scribbles and all the other puzzle pieces that Bruce was hoping would magically come together to tell the positive story of his life. His secretary Barb rolled her eyes as she handed me an accordion folder stuffed with a goulash of papers and notes. Frankly, it was a damned mess.

Bruce was in the same predicament I faced as a kid whenever a relative would buy me a model plane set for Christmas. I would open the package, parts would be everywhere, and all I knew was that I wanted that pretty looking airplane on the box cover to somehow come together and end up on the headboard of my bed. The process of assembling it would have to be done under the direction of somebody else because I was just not mechanically inclined. Now Bruce being the bright guy that he is, he quickly recognized that the assembler in the matter of his book needed to be me. And thus we struck a deal that led to the collection of words and thoughts and emotions you hold in your hands.

Every writing collaboration requires that the co-conspirators find a rhythm that works for both of them. Having written books in partnership with a well-known touring professional golfer; an artistic, mother-of-four cancer survivor; and a world-famous aerial photographer, I can tell you this is not always an easy task. But with Bruce it was effortless. We decided we would meet at least once a week in his office, where I would interview him on tape, and then shape his words into a narrative that would chronicle the events of his life — the good, the bad, and the ugly — but mostly the good. And that is because the Bruce Layne story is one of achievement and success, of a man overcoming early struggles, always keeping his chin up and eyes straight ahead, and through perseverance and hard work and clear thinking building the largest private insurance agency in the state of Nevada. But Bruce's story is far more than that. It's having and nurturing a great family, and never sloughing off the obligations of matrimony and parenthood. And it's about paying his civic rent to the community of Las Vegas every inch of the way. And of course it's a story that includes his most recent battle, the one against an adversary named Parkinson, and how at a point in his life when it appeared Bruce had cleared every significant hurdle, one more huge one was placed in front of him with the daunting challenge that screamed: "See how you handle this one, Big Boy!"

Before we plunged into the task of telling his story, I explained to Bruce the importance of answering two critical questions that every writer must address before the opening bell. 1) What is the thesis of the book? Basically, this means what is its purpose and message. And 2) Who is the audience for the book?

Bruce told me the purpose of the book was to provide a legacy of information for his children and grandchildren, and to impart the wisdom of his 58 years to anyone in his family or large group of friends and business associates who was interested. And so by answering the first question, we partially answered the second. Our audience was basically a group we'll call the Bruce Layne Fan Club. I offer this title in hindsight, because I can't imagine too many individuals who would number their "close circle of friends" at 50 to 100 people. I think after reading them you'll agree that the tributes and encomiums we gathered are as positive and sincere as any well-meaning person could ever hope to gather.

Another theme that was important to Bruce was the concept of *Paying It Forward*, the idea developed in a recent movie where by performing acts of kindness and generosity a person could create a ripple effect that would make the world a better place. This book, even before it was published, has done that. Don Doyle, Bruce's friend in San Francisco, not only started interviewing his father for his own memoirs, but he gave some early chapters of our book to a friend dying of multiple sclerosis, and it was very helpful to him. And after Bruce helped a fellow "Parkie" named Jim Williams up in Hayden Lake, Idaho, come to terms with his disease, Jim has become a morale booster for fellow sufferers in his area. And when you read Mike Hastings' comments, you'll find that Bruce's example as a hustling high school basketball player who rarely got to play in actual games was helpful to Mike when he was struggling with his career at a major college.

I know Bruce looks forward to hearing dozens of stories like these in future years as a result of writing this book.

I have joked with Bruce often in recent months that if the tables were turned and he were writing *my* life story, he might have a tough time finding half a dozen people to offer sincere tributes. Oh, he could find a flock of smart-asses, but people who would dig deep to "eulogize" me while I was still on their radar screen might be embarrassingly small in number. He'd dismiss such self-effacement with a comment like, "Ah, you're just a cynical Irishman," or he'd deride himself as a "friend slut." But make no mistake. While it's true that most of us can count our true, friend-in-need allies on one hand, the number of people Bruce Layne can honestly call "close friends" is several dozen. I know because I've spoken to all of them.

With each writing assignment I choose to take in my fourth decade as a professional scribbler, I hope to learn something interesting and enriching. If I were to headline the lessons I've learned in my dialogues with Bruce, it would be: "A Prescription for a Full and Rewarding Life." By hanging around this gentle man — note the separation between those two words — I've acquired the tools to become a better husband, a better father, and a better friend. I'm proud to say that I've added a close friend as well. And that's not an easy admission for a crusty Irishman.

— Jack Sheehan

Chapter 1

The Big Picture

I suppose the best piece of wisdom I've gotten from Bruce came from his baseball days at UNLV. He said, "You can't go through life with mitts on. You have to be able to throw something back." — Pam Newell

I first got the idea to put together my memoirs when I was at the beach a few months ago. There's something so peaceful and serene about the ocean that it can get a person thinking about larger issues that are easy to ignore amidst the mundane pursuits of everyday life. I began pondering what I could do with my time that would really be worthwhile.

I had been tremendously impressed by the message of the movie *Pay It Forward*. The movie dares to imagine doing a favor for someone and telling that person not to pay it back, but to pay it forward to three other people who, in turn, each pay it forward to three more. The result in an ideal world would turn into a global outpouring of kindness and decency. I just love that concept and have thought about it at length ever since I saw the film. It occurred to me that by writing a book to give to my friends and family, I could maybe pass on some lessons and philosophy I've developed through my own life that would in a sense Pay It Forward to all those I cared about. I have plenty of money and time on my hands, so I just started jotting down notes on what I had accomplished in my life. I started with the business and financial things, then the community involvement,

and I was frankly overwhelmed by how much I had achieved

But then I got angry with myself because it dawned on me that I hadn't taken the time to really savor what I'd accomplished. It was like this neon sign was flashing over my head that said, "You didn't appreciate it enough!" I guess I'd been going so fast through the years that I just took too many things for granted. Now I'm not one of those husbands/fathers who look back and scold themselves about not spending enough time with the wife and kids. I feel I've enjoyed a wonderful amount of time being attentive to Sherry and Chad and Trevor. I have great relationships with both of my sons, and we've always spent a good amount of time taking vacations together, just one at a time to get to know them better as individuals, and so I have no regrets there. But I hadn't really given enough thought to all the neat things I'd done outside of the family.

So "appreciation" and "savoring" became big words in my list of future priorities, and I felt that by writing down what I'd done in my life and how much it meant to me, I could come to a greater appreciation of it all. So the whole project grew partially out of a desire to reflect on all the aspects of my life for which I was

Chad, Bruce, Sherry and Trevor

grateful, and to create a meaningful legacy for my children and grandchildren.

The old axiom about not appreciating something until it's gone really hits home when a normal dumb guy like me gets hit with Parkinson's Disease. It's like getting struck by lightning. A huge sense of vulnerability overwhelms you, and you get that look-over-the-edge that is equal parts frightening and illuminating. I know my friend Freddie Albrecht looked at life differently after his cancer scare. He started to appreciate all the beautiful things in his life much more.

When the two-by-four hits you between the eyes you reach a level of immersion in the life process that is amazing. You experience a profound enlightenment. You cling to every moment. You hug your wife tighter, and your kids and your grand kids, and every moment with them takes on increased significance. The question becomes: Why can't we reach this level of savoring without being hit with a disease, or going through the terrorist attacks of 9/11, or

Bruce and Sherry in London 1978

A Touch of Zen

Jack Sheehan shared an anecdote with me about a Buddhist monk who falls over a cliff, and on his plunge to a certain death he reaches out to a branch growing out of the wall of the cliff. He clutches it momentarily, which breaks his fall, but it's clear that the branch is not strong enough to save him. As the roots pull out from the wall, the monk notices a buttercup growing at the base of the branch, and as the sun glistens off the petals, the monk appreciates in his dying moment the glory of the flower. The monk's very last thought before falling to his death is one of gratitude that he could experience this final moment of beauty. Now that is what I would call having great perspective.

facing a life-altering crisis? If I can raise everyone's appreciation for life and its special moments, then this memoir will be especially worthwhile.

I think the real gem out of this whole Parkinson's trip is that, although it is a progressive disease, I now have an even more relentlessly positive attitude than before, and I've learned how to take satisfaction to a higher level. These last four years have been a journey toward contentment, a living in the now, and a seizing of the moment.

People in business often spend so much time accumulating money, or building a portfolio, that it greatly reduces the savoring experience. Johnny Carson said years ago when he signed a huge contract to continue with *The Tonight Show* that money just provided another problem: what to do with it and how to manage it. Sherry and I have discussed how when we were struggling early on we were every bit as happy as today because we were trying to realize our goals and we had a pathway to follow. It's all about the journey and not the destination. Oh, the money buys you a little bit of freedom, but only in a material sense, not with emotional or spiritual matters.

The Big Deal

When we made the big deal and Brown and Brown bought Layne & Associates on July 3, 2001, for an eight-figure sum, there was an obvious letdown immediately afterward. Naturally, we celebrated the deal, and I felt a huge sense of relief that I wouldn't be sued and put out of business by some lawsuit or legal maneuver, but then a whole new set of insecurities started to creep in. What was my purpose now? What was my worth?

him what he was going to do after football, he said, "I have no idea." She replied, "Jerry, you're going to be miserable in retirement."

And she was correct, unless he can find a passion or a pursuit that equates in some way with his commitment to football.

So I have tried to find different interests. Like my mom, I've gotten into art, and I took an art class at UNLV taught by a long-time friend. I've read several books on art and have been to half a dozen museums including the Hermitage in Russia. And we've done some collecting. We have six lithographs from Chagall, and a Picasso and some Salvador Dali's. It is such an adjustment from the pace I was on, and changes are always tough. Sherry was concerned before we sold the company that I would have nothing else to do, but I have found a lot to keep me

When something that takes up 80 percent of your life is suddenly gone and all your duties change, it's scary. People who put all their value and self-esteem into their business are going to be in trouble if they don't find worthwhile outlets. I saw an interview recently with the great wide receiver Jerry Rice in which he talked about how he had been 100 percent committed to excellence as a football player since he was in high school. When the interviewer asked

Bruce, Sherry and the boys swimming 1976 (above). Bruce and Sherry and the boys in front of fireplace (right).

busy. For 35 years I had waked up early and left for work at 7 a.m. with my mind whirling around all the problems I would face that day and that constant knot in the stomach. During the drive to work I was figuratively putting my battle gear on to face the day. But I have found since the sale that I greatly enjoy those peaceful hours between 7:30 and 9:30 a.m., those wonderful times in the morning when I can relax and read the paper or a book. The view from our home of Red Rock and the Sheep Mountains is something I didn't truly appreciate until the last two years. We live in the southwest part of town at an elevation of almost 3,000 feet, about 1,000 feet higher than the valley floor, and there are mornings I just sit and soak it all in. It is so liberating.

I've heard people refer to retirement as a form of death, as a withdrawal from the vibrancy of living at a fast pace. Well, let me tell you what I'll miss about it. (*Tongue firmly planted in cheek*). I think I'll miss the rejection the most. In the insurance business you occasionally have to cold call and the person won't take the call or they tell you off, or they take your better quote and give it to their existing agent for leverage. That's always fun. And I miss the worry, the waking up at 2:30 in the morning and wondering whether I can make payroll, or worrying whether I'm going to write this account or keep that account. And of course I'll miss dealing with those attorneys and having the fear that I'm going to have some litigation and end up losing the whole company. Yeah, I'll miss all those wonderful aspects of work. So I have to say I haven't had any separation anxiety since selling the company. Actually, at the time of the deal I was battle weary.

Two days after the sale, on July 5th, we were on a cruise to the Baltics and Russia and Germany, and Chad called and said, "Dad, the Brown and Brown stock has gone way up. You made $1.1 million today." He had calculated it. And so I knew that I had made the right decision. And I felt that I had walked away at the right time, when our reputation was at its highest point.

I'd always worried about being like Willie Mays and hanging around too long, not knowing that my time was up.

Bruce and Sherry

14

Chapter 2

The Early Years in Las Vegas

My dad has shown me that the more obstacles we face, the stronger we will become,
and that we learn our most valuable lessons from our worst defeats and failures. — Trevor Layne

Our family moved here in March, 1955. I was just shy of 10 years old at the time. I was in the fourth grade, and I started at St. Anne's Grade School. I had been born in Los Angeles, but my family moved here because my mother liked the excitement of Las Vegas, and my grandmother thought it was a good idea, too. She was a real character. I'll have much more to say about her later.

My dad was a chiropractor in Hermosa Beach, and the women finally just harassed him into moving to Las Vegas. The population at the time here was something like 25,000 residents. I think starting a new practice for Dad here was a secondary consideration behind the fact that my mother and grandmother just wanted more action in their lives and they thought Las Vegas could provide it. And Dad just went along. He had been raised on a farm in Kansas, with a population of about

5,000, and my mom grew up in Los Angeles. My grandmother owned a couple of apartment buildings, and my dad was a tenant and met Mom there. They were married when she was just 16 years old and he was 19 or 20. People did that back then.

She had her first child, Jimmy, when she was just 17, and she was 19 when I was born. I didn't find it traumatic to move here. Remember, I was the second child, which means you're just happy to get a hug occasionally. The first kid has five thousand pictures taken of him, and the next one maybe three, and the third one two, and then the parents have a fourth baby years later and that baby gets spoiled. Las Vegas, however, was an exciting adventure for me, and my early friendships kind of typify the history of Las Vegas. A big shot in those days was Marion Hicks, who owned the Thunderbird Hotel. He was actually a front for the Kansas

Bruce's father bottom right.   *Mimi, Bruce's grandfather Harley, and Irene.*

15

City mob, and he came out here by jumping a train. Now there was an interesting fellow.

Anyway, his son Johnny Hicks became a friend of mine right away in school. Johnny's birthday was April 2, the day before mine, and for his party he took the whole class to the floor show at the Thunderbird. I was in awe. Theresa Brewer performed, and the Lucky Strike girls from television, and Zazu Pitts. Those were big names at the time. The emcee was Barney Rollins, who used to work at the old Las Vegas Convention Center.

Johnny's family owned the Little Church of the West, in front of the Algiers Hotel, and they gave Johnny $2,000 a month when he was in high school allegedly to run the place. So when we were just 14 or 15 Johnny would be running around with $2,000 in his pocket, always in cash, and by the time he was a senior he started hanging out with older guys and prostitutes. Later on, he was messing around with Lefty Rosenthal's wife Geri, who was played by Sharon Stone in the movie *Casino*. She ended up committing suicide years later in a motel in California. And Johnny was murdered when he was just 28 years old, shot by two people with silencers in the Green's Apartment at the Las Vegas Country Club.

Coming of Age

I remember an x-rated story concerning Johnny. I was either 12 or 13 at the time, and it was the first time I ever saw a naked woman. We were down at the Balboa Bay Club in Southern California; his dad had this 60-foot yacht, and Johnny asked me to go with him. We were there for about a week. After about three days his dad disappeared in his boat and we were left there at the club, which is a pretty hotsy-totsy place. This seemed pretty cool for two kids to have this kind of freedom, but after a couple of days we started getting scared. We were in the hotel, and we had room service and everything comped. Our room looked right out over the docks. After about the fourth day

we heard all of this ruckus down by the dock. It sounded like a wild party, so we snuck down there. And there was Marion Hicks with a couple other guys and about 10 naked women. So that was sort of the end of my innocence, right there. Johnny and I at first were shocked, and then we realized that this was kind of neat. So I guess you could say that primer course in sex education gave me a pretty fast introduction to Las Vegas.

I learned to play baseball in Las Vegas, and started in Little League right away. I remember when I was 12 I led the league in hitting with an average around .620. I was a left-handed shortstop, and a pretty good fielder.

Our home environment the first few years here was pretty stable. My dad was the nice guy and my mother was the "bad cop." She was always the disciplinarian, more demanding, and sometimes overbearing. I would even tell her that. She is even today a strong lady and has a lot of firm convictions about things. I remember she once washed out my mouth with soap. It was the worst thing you could ever experience. I was 10 or 11 at the time and my gums were sore for three

Bruce and Johnny Hicks

days. I'm sure it kept me from dropping the "F-bomb" more often.

I sensed that my mother and father were having some problems between them, but I didn't really know what it meant. They had split up a couple summers earlier as a trial separation, but I don't remember much fighting. I guess the cause of the breakup was that my mother wanted more excitement. She wanted more parties and more out of life, and Dad was kind of a homebody.

I knew he was drinking too much, and later on that would really become a problem, but I think the drinking really didn't occur until after they split up. A lot of people in Las Vegas get seduced by the gambling, and I know he liked to gamble. So did my grandmother. She was a wheeler-dealer. She fancied herself an expert in astrology, and she would come up with certain colors and go gambling at certain times when she felt the stars were aligned right, and she would wear certain perfumes she thought were lucky. What a character! I remember she loved the Horseshoe Club in particular.

The Family Splits Up

I don't remember any particular dramatic moment where my parents sat us down and told us they were getting divorced, but my mother

did talk to me and she told me that she expected me to go back to California with her. I was almost 16 at the time, in my sophomore year at Gorman High School. I did not want to leave all of my friends. My mom was going to leave the Las Vegas house and Dad was going to stay there. She was moving to San Francisco. I remember how upset my dad was and I felt sorry for him, and that is another reason I wanted to stay with him. At the time Jimmy was away at college, Long Beach State, and my two younger brothers were going with Mom. She gave me a hard time about staying in Las Vegas, but I just said, "No, I think Dad needs me." I just couldn't bear the thought of his losing his entire family. And so I stayed.

It seemed fine for a while, but then my dad started drinking too much. When I was 18 Tim was shipped back to my dad here in Las Vegas because he was having problems in California, and I ended up taking care of him about two-thirds of the time. It was not a very good environment for him with Dad and me. Dad had this degenerate girlfriend named Pearl who was living with us. She had some kind of accounting job, but she was a real floozy and it was a terrible environment for Tim. I told Dad what I thought about it and he kicked me out of the house. So I took Tim with me. We lived in an apartment over on Maryland Parkway, for about $75 a month. I was working and just about to start at UNLV. I was a bus boy at the Thunderbird and then later a lifeguard at the Riviera Hotel pool.

That was a tough time for us. I was still uncertain about my goals, and here I was acting as the surrogate father for a six year old. I had to grow up pretty quickly, and I found that when you're in a survival mode you do what you have to do to get along.

Dad was really unhappy that I'd taken Tim from him, and at one point he said he was going to put the FBI on me. Bob Miller, who would later serve as a two-term District Attorney for Clark County and a two-term Nevada Governor,

Tim, Jeff, and Mimi

17

told me shortly afterward that I might have been vulnerable to charges had they been filed. I could have been nailed for kidnapping, but I was doing what I felt to be right at the time.

Eventually, Dad and I worked out our problems and ended up having a good relationship. He was, after all, a genuinely good and kind person, and I'd be remiss if I didn't emphasize the good will and virtues that he passed on to his sons. His philosophy was always that we should look for a person's best qualities rather than emphasize the failings. In hindsight, I owe a lot to Sherry for her intervention in helping Dad and me close what I'll call the "Timmy wound."

Brotherly Love

I'm not sure of the length of time — Timmy says it's three years — but he eventually went back to California to live with Mom. I do think he truly appreciates the sacrifices I had to make to watch over him during that difficult period of time. Despite his tough upbringing, he has grown into

Tim, Irene, Jim, Jeff, and Bruce

a wonderful adult. He earned a degree from Long Beach State and became an outstanding naval architect. He has a loving family with two great children. Tim was a member of the San Francisco Yacht Club, where he raced sailboats, and is building his own boat after losing the first one in a terrible storm that broke up the marina.

Around the same time that Tim left for California, my older brother Jimmy started having serious problems. He had joined the military, and he had a nervous breakdown while he was stationed at Fort Bliss in Texas. We never found out the exact details. We know he made it through basic training all right, and then something happened and the Army gave him

Tim's sail boat

electric-shock treatments that fried his brain. Jimmy is still alive today and in good shape physically, but not mentally. He does remember dates and old memories of Las Vegas. But he has no emotions, sort of like the Dustin Hoffman character in *Rainman*. It was a real tragedy. He was a helluva guy, good looking and a good athlete. Mickey Falba was talking about him not long ago and he said Jimmy was the best hitter he ever saw in high school. Jimmy's best friends were Charlie Ruggeroli, the cardiologist, and Michael Gaughan, who owns the Coast hotels and casinos. Michael always asks me about Jimmy whenever I see him. Jimmy now lives with my brother Jeff in San Francisco. Jeff deserves a lot of credit for looking after him. Jim owns the house and still collects a pension from the Army, but boy did my mother have to fight for that! He doesn't spend much money, and the compounded interest from all his savings has given him a nice estate.

Anyway, when Jimmy came back to Las Vegas after the Army released him he was just wandering the streets. He could not take care of himself. He was a homeless guy before we had a lot of homeless people. This was very heavy stuff for me, to see my older brother in that kind of shape. One time the cops had to get him. They handcuffed him and put him in University Medical Center. It was a jail situation where he was in confinement. I remember I had to go to court to get them to commit him to the state mental institution in Sparks. That was traumatic as hell, to have to do that, but it was the right thing for him. He has never forgiven me to this day for doing that, but what other choice was there? My mom was not going to take him — she had a new husband by then — nor was my dad in any condition to take on that responsibility. And shortly afterwards, in 1971, my dad died.

I don't know how long they kept Jimmy at Sparks. That's all kind of foggy to me, but my mom would know. Later on she took responsibility, and she has been really good to him through the years. Mom is a classy lady: strong, outspoken, and tough, but she dies a death every day in dealing with Jimmy. You know the Army never takes responsibility for these kinds of cases, but my mother fought like a junk yard dog to get Jimmy the benefits he deserved. She went to all the U.S. Senators in California and fought with the Veterans Administration and she got him put in a halfway house, where he lived for years. But he got temperamental and combative, so they kicked him out of about three placements.

Jimmy is not able to hold down a job and never spends a dime, which is why he has accumulated all that money. Today he is kind of like a hippie. He is still a hell of an athlete, and he bowls and plays golf, but he also talks to himself and is schizophrenic. His quality of life is, of course, very limited.

Growing Pains

I wasn't much of a fighter in school, but I know my brother Jeff recalls a time when I popped a guy at a stoplight after he and his friend had flipped me off when I had kids in the car. And there was a time I remember during my junior year at Gorman when I was at this Spudnuts shop. They don't have them anymore. I would get this cheese sandwich and put it in a lunch

Tim, Bruce, Jeff, and Jim

Tim and Irene

bag for school. It was always cheese because it was cheaper than the other sandwiches and I didn't have any money. Anyway, this guy named Carl Dotson, who was a senior, stole my lunch. So I challenged him to a fight and we arranged to meet in the Bryan Park area, near 15th and St. Louis Street. There was a park there, and about 200 witnesses showed up.

Bruce, R. J., and Bob Miller

Mimi, Jim, Tim, and Jeff

Sure enough, he drove up in this blue '55 Chevy, all customed-out, and he slammed on his brakes and slid out of the car. Think of a greasy character like Sal Mineo in *Rebel Without a Cause* and you'll have a good picture of Carl.

Just as he started to take off his coat, I nailed him. I always knew to get in the first punch. And I was getting the best of him, when all of a sudden he reversed it and had me on the ground and was getting the best of me. Just then somebody yelled "Cops!" And everyone ran off, including Carl. I was so happy. Whoever yelled might have saved my life.

Other jobs I had growing up were as a soda jerk and a lifeguard at the Riviera Hotel swimming pool, thanks to Bob Miller's dad Ross. I was also a P.E. coach at St. Christopher's, where one of my players was a kid named Billy Young, who was recently elected Sheriff of Clark County.

I also delivered subpoenas for Clark County. Several people said they wanted to kick my ass after I handed them the subpoena. Another time I was working at a bank and I had to go and get Dart Anthony's credit card repo'd. People might remember him as the animal-rights activist who rescued Donna the Duck from the pond at Sahara Golf Course. That was the duck that some juvenile delinquent had shot with an arrow that stuck through her. The duck's picture appeared in about every national magazine. Naturally when a flamboyant guy named Dart saves a seriously wounded Duck, huge publicity is sure to follow. But the truth is the guy was a marginal character and the newspapers even called him a scam artist.

I also earned money working as a Shamrock usher for old man Mulroy, whose daughter-in-law Pat runs the Water District. (You can see from all the name-dropping that at one time Las Vegas was indeed a small town.) Basically, I did what I had to do to get by.

Bruce, Tim, and Jeff

Chapter 3
Discovering the Real World: Fear Strikes Out

Although women are usually better at sizing up people than men, Bruce has a keen woman's intuition about people. — Craig Sullivan

When I was working at the titanium plant after flunking out of college, Chub Drakulich, the Nevada Southern (now UNLV) baseball coach, came to me and urged me to go back to school. What caused him to do this, I'm not certain I'll ever know, but fate certainly had a hand in it. I was just miserable working at the plant. I hated the hours, the lack of meaningful conversation on my breaks, even the grease that got under my fingernails. I went to bed every night with a gut-wrenching fear that I was going to end up a total dud, never reaching anything close to my potential. When Chub told me he wanted me back and that he would get me a scholarship, it was like someone turned the light back on. "If the genes fit, wear 'em!" he preached. I instinctively sensed that this was the break I needed. Career-wise, I look at that moment as the major turning point in my life. I knew that I had to take over the responsibility for maximizing my own potential. I returned to school and the baseball team and worked my tail off in school and on the baseball diamond. The first time I had enrolled I had no focus and no direction. I did not have pride of workmanship. My first report card showed 17 hours of D, no C's

TOP REBEL HITTER--Bruce Layne, Nevada Southern first baseman, presently leads Rebels in hitting with batting average near .600. He has hit in past five Rebel games, and hit seven times straight in his last seven at bats. Layne will start against Weber State in a doubleheader Saturday, starting at 12 noon on the campus field. NSU's Easter Tournament begins March 21. (Photo courtesy of Las Vegas Review Journal)

and no F's. It was a 1.0 grade average that was accompanied by a letter from the registrar that basically gave the old umpire call: "You're outta here!" So I was determined to do better when I got that "life mulligan," and I did. I think it's happily ironic that I eventually became one of UNLV's strongest alumni supporters, the only alumnus on the Foundation Board from 1985 to 1995.

I finally earned my economics degree from UNLV in 1969 — I like to call it the six-and-a-half year program without the doctorate — and it had always occurred to me that once I got a real job it would be forever. I wasn't ready for "forever" at that point, so I put off that monumental decision and took a part-time job at Quali-Craft Shoes, a chain outlet selling shoes to women. As *Married With Children's* Al Bundy would attest, the money wasn't great, but the job had its perks. It was at that job, though, where I learned the art of persuasion.

When a 300-pound lady would come in with gunboats size 12 and ask for a size 7, you quickly learned the skills of tact and persuasion. Great care was required to avoid offending the customer. I liked the old shoe-stretcher, which was the end of a broomstick that could help a size seven expand to a size nine. The objective was very simple: sell shoes and don't hurt the customer's feelings.

I also had a part-time job on the midway at Circus Circus for several months. And then I got my first serious job at Valley Bank, which was known back then as the Bank of Las Vegas. One of the bank executives named Herb Stout gave me the job. As I recall, I made $525 per month as a management type person, just learning the business. But the thing that drove me out of that career was that I did not like having to be there all the time. The nine-to-five, five-day-a-week aspect really got to me. I liked the flexibility of working until midnight tonight and taking off and going skiing tomorrow. I have never been one who liked too much structure in a job, and I think that has always allowed me to think outside the box. And that was one reason I got interested in the insurance business. I had spoken with my good friend Tito Tiberti's father, J.A., who encouraged me in that direction.

A great opportunity occurred when Don Harris, who was working for Cragin and Pike Insurance Company, ended up going to Marsh and McLennan and hired me. I went to Los Angeles to be trained. This was in 1970 and '71. Marsh and McLennan was then, and still is, the world's largest insurance broker. I received great training over there, and I ended up getting what is considered a master's degree in insurance, the CPCU, which is a prestigious credential. Sherry had always bugged me about the insurance business's having a terrible image, and that motivated me to get the CPCU even though it required about 20 hours a week of extra study. It was that training that helped me, in later years, figure out ways for Las Vegas hotel-casinos to revolutionize the way they bought insurance, by getting large deductibles and self-insuring. I also designed a template for their handling of claims that allowed the hotels to cut their losses by 50 percent. Anyway, I worked for Marsh and McLennan for a while and then was hired

by Cash, Sullivan, and Cross in 1973. They did all of the Del Webb Company's insurance. I opened an office for them here in Las Vegas.

My Big Break

I ran that office for over 10 years, and we ended up with $500,000 in commission income and five employees. I then made an offer to buy them out, in August of 1984, for $167,000 over five years; they accepted the offer. Those guys at Cash Sullivan were wonderful people, and they were more than fair with me because back then an insurance business was probably worth just what its annual commissions were: they sold the business to me for a third of that because they knew that I had generated all the income. That was yet another compassionate act by good people, which in turn made me more compassionate in business. And that was the beginning of Layne & Associates, the company that would really bring all my success in Las Vegas. By the time we sold to Brown and Brown in 2001, our five employees had grown to 80 and our commissions had exploded from $500,000 to $6.8 million annually.

I didn't realize how differently people treat you when you own a company and have your name on the door. Shortly after buying it I was awarded the Distinguished Alumni Award from UNLV; pretty ironic considering I had basically flunked out of there on my first go-round 20 years before. Suddenly, with Layne & Associates, I had my own identity, my own niche in the business world, and that gave me a desire to get more involved in the community. It seemed through the next several years that I was the president of about 49 different organizations. And the more I gave to the community, and the more involved I became in charitable causes, the more business came to us. But I didn't give all this time to the Chamber and to Kiwanis and to the community because it was self-serving. I did it because it was the right thing to do. Outside of work habits and discipline and all that, I would cite community involvement as the single most important aspect of our growing this company as big as we did. Networking and doing good works for the community just enhances your credibility. Because I acknowledged and understood that the insurance industry doesn't have the greatest reputation, I felt it was imperative that I show people I was honest and involved and could be trusted.

On a side note, my success in the insurance business was a springboard to other opportunities, such as real estate investment. I had gotten tired of hearing all those Vegas sob stories of how people had passed on land-buying opportunities that would have provided them financial freedom. So with some of my closest friends, I started an investment club called Sunride Investments. Our initial $5,000 investment, which was accrued by collecting $50 monthly payments from several people, is today worth over $1 million. I had the attitude then that I would let others talk about the ones that got away, and I would go out and get them.

Some Keys to Success

I'm often asked how we built our company, and it's never a simple answer. It was a combination of a lot of different elements. While I believe that the most important element of success is customer service, the customer comes second. And that's because your employees should come first. If you treat your employees first rate, that level of service will be passed on to the customer.

In those early years we had a frenetic annual growth rate of $2.5 million of additional premiums per year, and to do that we had to have people who had a good attitude and were self-sufficient.

It's really sort of a relentless assault that involves marketing, great sales techniques, being visible in the community, and being available,

having friends provide entrees to other friends, and then, as the company grows, learning how to delegate a lot of the work to strong employees. In the beginning it even involves knocking on doors of people who don't know you, and being able to withstand the rejection. To succeed in sales, you have to learn not to take it personally.

I remember having a job right after college where I sold *Grolier's Encyclopedias* for six months. That was quite an experience. There was a family whose door I knocked on out at Nellis Air Force Base. A lady came to the door and said, "Yes, can I help you?" And I said, "I'm Bruce Layne and I am here to sell you some encyclopedias. I can see that you have three children in there, and I think it's very important that they have access to all this information."

And she was very pleasant and invited me in and I talked to her for five or 10 minutes telling her all of the virtues of these books, and she finally said, "I really don't think that I can afford another set of encyclopedias. We bought a set just last year and our kids are using them now." And she pointed toward the kids and I could see that they were sitting on the books watching cartoons. They were using them as chairs. Selling doesn't get much tougher than that. I think I sold two sets during the entire time with Grolier's.

The Least-Read Best-Seller

The only time I ever got fired was from a company called Delta Maintenance. I worked the midnight to eight a.m. shift cleaning public rest rooms for J.C. Penny stores in downtown Las Vegas. I remember watching the owner pick up a sanitary screen from a urinal and cleaning it with her hands. When she fired me after three days she said she was letting me go because, and I quote, "Your heart is not in your work." I remember saying to myself, "Thank God."

Getting back to insurance, it sounds corny, but like any other profession you have to work from the bottom up and learn the trade. And you have to take great pride in the workmanship. Through the years I came to enjoy insurance. It is a very technical business, but one that the average citizen pays little attention to. For that reason a broker must pay *great* attention to it. The saying goes that an insurance policy is America's number-one least-read best-seller. The insurance industry does a terrible job in educating the public on what they really do. When you see these huge judgments that juries give out to people, and the average citizen applauds, he or she doesn't seem to realize whose pocketbook it will ultimately affect. You see it today with these huge tobacco settlements. It's easy to root against the tobacco companies and for the poor lady with lung cancer and award her family $18 million, but it's the consumer who ends up paying that judgment. When I started to learn the business I wanted to cut myself out of the herd of sleazy insurance salesmen, and that's why I spent five years studying and taking national exams to get that CPCU designation. There are probably only eight or 10 of us in the city of Las Vegas who have that.

I always tried to make Layne & Associates a cut above. We once had a survey taken, and we found out that our image was actually much better than the reality of our company. Our image was incredible, but that's because our performance was so strong that it resulted in 98 percent retention of clients from year to year. Average in the industry is about 65 percent. And I was proud to be the hood ornament of that image.

Bruce, Tito and Bob Miller

If I were to assess my strengths in business it would not be that I'm necessarily good with numbers. It's more of an analytical ability. I've always been able to analyze financial statements and make sense of them. And I have an ability to administrate. I have a pretty good feel for what makes people tick and how I can motivate them. I'm also a good listener and can be empathetic to people's problems and situations. Everybody has a different style, and mine is to really talk to people and occasionally listen to whining and sniveling so that I can get at the root of a problem, then treat the person with compassion and fairness. I think anyone who has worked for me recognizes my attention to loyalty to employees and sensitivity to their problems. They've always known that I have an open-door policy and that they can talk to me. Sometimes I marvel that we grew Layne & Associates from a five-person business to over 80 employees with what I like to call an organized chaos. But we did.

Insurance is far more of an emotional sale than an intellectual sale. For years I misled myself by thinking that people would buy because I was a great technician. But it really comes down to being likeable. People have to like any vendor they are buying from. The trust factor is enormous in any sale. When we did that client survey through UNLV a few years ago and 250 of our clients filled out questionnaires, 92 percent said trustworthiness was the more important attribute they looked for in an insurance agent, and 91 percent said that they would rank Layne & Associates either "good" or "excellent" as being trustworthy. That is probably the essence of our success right there. And those were very gratifying numbers.

Role Models

If you asked me to name a role model in business, believe it or not the first name that would come to mind is my grandmother's. Lois Henderson, whom we called Grandma Mimi, was 95 when she died five years ago, and she shared more insight and intuition with me than anyone. She was really a mystical person. She could talk about business, spiritual things, medicine, you name it. She left her husband when she was 42 years old and went to chiropractic school. She used to drive around the country by herself. I would go to her for advice for my business, right up to the day she died. No one did more than my grandmother to instill self-esteem in me. Many times she would take my hand and look me in the eye and say, "You are special, Brucie." And this wasn't just when I was a little boy. This was when I was well into my 40s with children who were young adults.

Bruce's father-in-law, Bill Borellis

My father-in-law, Bill Borellis, was a pilot and a war hero. He flew 35 missions over Germany during World War II. I had a close relationship with him; in fact I think I may be the only person who knew that he had always had a secret desire to be an actor. He certainly had the looks for it — he resembled a swashbuckling Errol Flynn. He was an accomplished architect with an eye for beauty.

And I have to credit my two lifelong friends, Tito Tiberti and Bob Miller. Tito was kind of a moral compass and a great sounding board for me. He's a strong willed, virtuous guy, highly principled, and that made a big impression on me. I remember a two-week period when I was just out of school and I was holding down two jobs, at Valley Bank and at the Stardust Hotel swimming pool. Occasionally, I'd cop out of some of my bank responsibilities for which I was being paid and go work at the pool. Basically, I was double dipping. I told Tito about it in a bragging sort of way, and he said, "That's wrong. It's like stealing." He really scolded me and I never forgot that.

With Bob Miller, it's his determination that has always impressed me. He is focused and tenacious. Growing up, you wouldn't think Bob would end up being a two-term governor. Even though he was an honest, no impropriety, no-nonsense guy, he took a lot of kidding because he was the tallest kid around and very uncoordinated. One time in the eighth grade he broke his leg, and then the next year he took a swing at a kid named Herbie Snyder, and broke his hand. Shortly after that, he broke his arm, so he had a cast on his hand and his leg at the same time. I also remember one time playing against Boulder City in a Jayvee game, Bob got the ball on a tip-off and spun around and made a fabulous shot. Unfortunately, it went in the wrong basket and he scored two for BC. He was just a terrible basketball player as a kid, but he worked on it and worked on it and ended up a very good player. And just recently, playing golf with Jack Sheehan (who would normally give Bob a stroke a hole for 18 holes), Miller shot a 40 on the front nine at Anthem Country Club and came within one stroke of tying Jack for that nine. I know he

25

was proud of that. So he has a tenacity that I have always admired, and I think a sizable number of Nevadans would regard him as a great governor, one of the best in our state's history.

I would also mention John F. Kennedy. He was young and bright and idealistic and it was a big thing for us Catholics to finally have a Catholic President.

There are countless other leaders on both local and national levels that are admirable, but there is one person who rises above all of them and has long been viewed as the greatest leader this nation has ever known; that is, of course, Abraham Lincoln. Lincoln's leadership was such that it is a model for future generations. He had a great understanding of human nature and a plain common-sense disposition and straightforward purpose that inspired people to believe in him and follow him. He was always guided by principle, yet had a compassion even in time of war that caused him to issue pardons and show great respect to the enemy. I highly recommend the book *Lincoln on Leadership* to everyone.

And then there's my all-time role model (*laughing*), John Derek. But there's an Alfred Hitchcock twist to this one. This is a guy who was married to perhaps the three most beautiful women in the world, Ursula Andress, Linda Evans, and Bo Derek, but they were all friends and they all came to his funeral and said how wonderful he was. Now for a guy to pull that one off well, that says something about the power of persuasion. He would have made a great insurance salesman.

Job Satisfaction

I've talked about the unsavory reputation the insurance industry has, but there's also a very rewarding side to it. And that happens when you settle claims for people and help them get their lives back in order, whether it be from a home fire or some other setback. And I enjoy those times when I have given good advice to people about the amount of protection or coverage they needed. When you're able to hand a large check to a widow from a life insurance policy and you've removed that financial burden that looms over her, that is very satisfying. People don't always take your advice, however. There was a time when I told a hotel owner at Stateline that the one million-dollar liability coverage he had was not nearly enough. They did not listen. The next month a little boy was murdered on their property, and they had to pay much more than that.

There was another instance in the 1980s when I told the executives at the Gold Strike Casino in Boulder City that they needed a helicopter company that was giving excursions out of the hotel to purchase separate insurance coverage. The purpose was to have the helicopter company additionally insured so that the responsibility for an accident was transferred to them. Wouldn't you know, about one month later a woman chasing a wind-blown hat was decapitated on the property. My advice in that case saved the hotel a huge loss.

One of the keys to this business is to handle situations pragmatically, and without getting too emotional. I've always been good at problem solving. I can look at a problem analytically and say, "Okay, this is what we need to do to get through this." I don't over-react. I guess I'm a chronic fixer. I like to fix things, whether it is people's feelings or problems, or a temporary crisis at work. It's so important to have dignity in the heat of battle. I've always admired resiliency in people, like the boxer who can take one punch after another and keep coming back because of an inner drive or the size of his heart. I like Evander Holyfield because he was never the most talented boxer, but he would never quit, and he found ways to win just through his courage and tenacity.

I suppose it is this characteristic, whether it's just in my DNA or my upbringing, I'm not really sure, that has served me well in my fight with Parkinson's disease. I'm not so much concerned with why it happened to me as how I can beat it and maintain quality of life in spite of it. I keep a postcard that Sherry gave me on my desk; it sums up something that she and I believe:

Life's Little Reminder

The journey has always been about laughing together, loving each other, seeking adventure, believing in our dreams and making a difference…but sometimes we forget…to enjoy the journey.

And on the other side it quotes Kobi Yamata: "Sometimes you just have to take the leap, and build your wings on the way down."

We have always in our 34 years together respected and nurtured each other's feelings. Bruce and I have been able to mix our love with an ability to be best friends. — Sherry Layne

Chapter 4

The Diagnosis

Bruce is not a blurry-eyed optimist who thinks everything will be just fine. He's too much of a realist for that, but he will treat this battle with courage and intelligence. — Tito Tiberti

I was diagnosed with Parkinson's disease on April 26, 1999.

I had been getting little hints from friends for several months that something was wrong, but I honestly didn't feel any different. Gov. Bob Miller, for one, was telling me that I was moving too slowly on the golf course. And my son Trev and I had finished golfing one day and he popped off and said, "Start moving faster, Old Man." And Tito Tiberti told me that he wanted me to go to Dr. Corey Brown and get a checkup, to make sure I was okay.

So I went to see Corey, it was on a Monday, and his exact words after looking at me were, "You're going to the neurologist." I asked him what he thought was wrong, and he said, "You either have a brain tumor or you have had a stroke or you have Parkinson's."

I was shocked that he would say that. Corey had merely asked me to walk up and down his hallway, but he didn't like what he was seeing. My left arm did not move properly and I was walking with a slight shuffle — sort of the old man shuffle — where you don't pick your feet up but sort of just slide along. But I have to say in hindsight I was unaware that these things were going on.

I went to the neurologist, Dr. Nicole Theuvenet, a couple days later and she told me after a few quick little tests that I definitely had Parkinson's. They don't test for the disease by taking MRIs or x-rays, and there is no standard test to show you that you have it. It's more like, "Okay, close your eyes and touch your nose," and "Okay now, bend your arm." Simple stuff like that. And after watching me go through some of these drills the doctor made her diagnosis. So there were now two physicians in different fields telling me that I had it. It was devastating.

Of course the initial shock was tough, and I was really depressed for about four days. In a short period of time I went through Elizabeth Kubler-Ross's five stages of death. There's the shock, then the denial, then the anger and resentment and self-pity — all of that junk. And immediately upon hearing the news I didn't know whether I had a week or a month or a year left to live. I'd been told it was incurable and progressive, and I thought maybe it would get so bad that dying would be a better fate than being wheelchair bound and without use of my faculties. Those were a dark few days.

But then I pulled out of it really quickly. I thought: All right, let's move forward and find out what we can about this and get back to my life. I'm proud that I didn't curl up into a ball and let it consume me, but then I've always been a pretty good battler. Giving up is just not the way I deal with things. However, I did have to absorb the reality of the situation for a while before I quickly got back to my old self.

The Fight Begins

As I started reading about it I realized how little is known about the disease. Parkinson's is a nerve disorder and a movement disorder wherein you lose your dopamine, and when you lose 80 percent of the dopamine that your nervous system transmits to the brain then your movements start changing. And then you can get dyskinesia, like Michael J. Fox has, where his arms and legs just all of a sudden shoot out violently. I learned that Parkinson's is a mysterious disease, yet one that afflicts over a million people in the United States, about one in every 300. Various estimates put the number of Parkinson's sufferers in Las Vegas at between 8,000 to 12,000 people.

Sherry was at a regional Arabian Horse Show in Scottsdale, where she was in charge of the whole thing, and I called her after meeting with Corey and of course she was immediately shocked and worried and came home to attend the neurologist's visit with me. When she left Arizona she told all her "horsey" friends why she needed to come home and that upset me because my first reaction was that I didn't want anyone to know. I was extremely self-conscious about my condition in the first weeks and months after the diagnosis. I have a lot of pride and I didn't want anyone's sympathy, and I especially didn't want anyone staring at me to see how I was doing.

Neither Sherry nor I are very dramatic people on the surface — she's an Annie Oakley type tough girl with her horses and all — but it really hit home when we got the news. All of the priorities of life started to fall into a clean order. Little things that would bug me before became totally insignificant, and the big things like family and kids and grand kids went right to the top of the list in capital letters. There's an instant fear of death combined with an enormous appreciation of life, and even in those first weeks following the news I felt a huge amount of gratitude for all that I'd been given in life — my family, my successful business, and the generally great health I'd enjoyed up until that point. I was 53 years old when I was diagnosed, and I think I'd missed about two days of work in my entire career. So not being perfectly healthy was going to require a lot of mental and physical adjustments.

I've read quite a bit and participated in studies and clinical trials on Parkinson's. One major study that I became a "reluctant astronaut" in was done by Yale University. In a six-month period I had 150 vials of blood taken and underwent 35 EKG's. Twenty out of 30 patients in that study got better. I was one that didn't because, as I learned later, I was in the control group taking a placebo. This was a very nervous time for me because I had no idea whether the stuff I was ingesting would cure me or kill me outright. It could have reacted like rat poison or anthrax for all I knew.

I now know that Parkinson's works differently in different people. I know people in Las Vegas that were diagnosed after I was and who are in much worse shape than me today. We know that it is a progressive disease, but there's no way of telling how it affects longevity. Some people do live out their full life span, although in a seriously diminished capacity. Attitude is everything, and it is the one thing about this disease that I *can* control. I just refuse to give in to the depression (not that I don't have down moods, because I do), but when I start feeling low I just try to do something positive for myself or someone else, and that helps snap me out of it.

A big part of my motivation to put my thoughts in writing was to pass on to my family and my precious grand kids information about my life, with its ups and downs, so they could hear from me in my own words exactly what happened to ol' Bruce Layne — the good, the bad, and the ugly. I also wanted to pass on a little wisdom and philosophy from my life and all its setbacks and triumphs, which is something I've done for years by speaking to youth groups on career-day forums (*more on this later*).

Getting back to the disease, it is very different from cancer and other illnesses in that there is no standard treatment. With cancer you know you have an option for surgery or radiation or chemotherapy, but with Parkinson's you're sort of out there in the ozone. It is a mystery. Nobody really knows how it works. They just know that you lose your dopamine, which is something that occurs naturally with aging but which is accelerated with Parkinson's. I've heard it said that if everyone lived to be 110 years old, everyone would have Parkinson's. So in that sense it's like a premature aging disease that moves at a hyper rate of speed. I don't know what else to say about it.

I immediately thought about dying when I got the diagnosis, and the sense of immortality we feel in our 20s and 30s was totally erased. But I will say that the fear of death is greatly lessened when you feel that you've accomplished something worthwhile and performed some good works on the planet. And I do feel I've created a positive legacy and made a difference, and that fact alone greatly reduces my fear of death.

The Man in the Mirror

About a week after getting the news I went back to work, but I was very self-conscious. I was always looking at my hands to see if they were shaking and if people were acting differently toward me. And I reflected on some rumors that had been circulating for the previous several months. Some people had heard that I had a stroke, and others were told that I had MS and was dying. And this made me realize that there were at least some of the symptoms of Parkinson's that had been evident to people as much as a year before. In fact, as we prepared this memoir, Tito told Jack Sheehan a story that really surprised me. Tito said that he and I were at lunch a year before my diagnosis, in April of 1998, and we ran into Dr. Gerry Sylvain, an eye doctor that we've both known forever, and that Gerry called him later that day and asked what was wrong with me. He had picked up on whatever symptoms were manifested at that time, and he was concerned. So if I were to guess today, in late 2002, I suppose

that the disease started creeping into my body maybe as early as 1996 or 1997.

I've come to appreciate that your health situation is like your financial situation. Money doesn't become a big worry or priority in your life unless you don't have any. And you don't think much about health when you're feeling great. But when you get something like Parkinson's, health leaps to the top of your worry list.

So when I went back to work I was determined to stay positive and press forward like I'd always done. I thought often about the lectures I'd given to kids on career days in Las Vegas — I've probably spoken to about 4000 kids on success and failure and how to get more satisfaction and fulfillment in life — and I just applied those principles to my own situation. Doing good things for others or for the community has always bolstered my spirits, so I resolved to do more of that. I quickly started to look at the disease as a gift that could make me a better, stronger person with a more clearly defined list of priorities.

One of the many frustrations with this disease is that my control over it is so limited. You know you are going to get worse; it's just a matter of how quickly and how bad it will get. I think my decline over the last four years has been gradual rather than rapid because by keeping a positive attitude I know I can nullify the downward trend. I need to stay as active as I can be. I am always reading the latest research and studies and keeping an eye open for cures and advancements. I'd like to find a drug that would help me calm the symptoms and be productive for longer periods of time, so I keep my eyes and ears open for any new developments or treatments.

Some of the articles I read are encouraging, and others are totally depressing. There was a recent article in the *Wall Street Journal*

(December 3, 2002) that really took the wind out of my sails. In part it read:

In a quiet disappointment for cell-based medicine, scientists have reported that a second large study of transplanted fetal cells has found no benefit for patients suffering from Parkinson's disease. The treatments also caused serious side effects.

"The results are a blow to hopes that infusions of brain tissue from aborted fetuses could reverse the degenerative brain condition, and may also dampen expectations for treatments using stem cells….

The patients received brain tissues from as many as eight fetuses, each approximately six to nine weeks old and the result of an abortion. Although brain scans showed that the transplanted cells appeared to be functioning normally, the researchers reportedly weren't able to find any measurable improvement in tests of motor and other skills.

"But the most severe setback was side effects such as uncontrolled motions of the limbs, which affected 13 of the 23 patients who received cells. Three of them had symptoms so severe they required an additional surgery to control them…"

Now when I read that report, I couldn't help but be depressed. So much hope for the cure for Parkinson's is tied to stem cell research that this news was like a hard kick to the stomach. But then just as fast as I get down, someone will point me to another article that suggests other cutting edge treatments are encouraging.

Here's a portion of a *Business Week* article that came out about the same time:

"For the victims of brain diseases, the golden hope is that scientists will figure out how to make damaged cells deep inside the brain regenerate. If this magic capability could be extended to the frayed neurons of patients suffering from Alzheimer's, stroke, Lou Gehrig's disease, or Parkinson's, their brains might restore themselves, much like skin that heals after a cut.

"For Parkinson's sufferers, this dream may be moving toward reality thanks to the revival of a drug written off as a failure just three years ago. A clinical trial at the University of Kentucky is currently treating 10 Parkinson's patients with a bioengineering protein, called GDNF, using a radical new drug-delivery method that sends it deep into the part of the brain where Parkinson's originates. There, a constant supply is administered by a pump implanted in the chest. So far, GDNF seems both to shield healthy brain cells from the disease and cause damaged cells to regenerate.

"'After just a few months of testing,' says Kentucky investigator Greg Gerhardt, 'there is evidence of improvement in patients.' In addition, British doctors reported last April that a similar trial in Bristol, England, improved muscle control of all five patients tested within a month of treatment."

Needless to say, when I read this second article, my heart — to quote Chief Dan George in the movie *Little Big Man* — soared like an eagle. So the news is bad one day and good the next. All I can do is stay on top of the research and the learning curve.

In November of 2002 I had my medicine upgraded because my tremor was getting worse and my gait was getting choppier. I was dragging my left foot more than before. So they added a drug called Amantadine to my regimen. And I've recently started taking Seniment, which Michael J. Fox has been on for years. He's even gone to the extreme measure of having a Pallidotomy, an operation in which a part of the globus pallidus is destroyed. They put your head in a metal cage during that one. It doesn't sound very enticing.

Another symptom I've been having since the fall of '02, which is a side effect of the medications, is that I experience hallucinations. I can laugh about it and say, like that little boy in the movie

The Sixth Sense, "I see dead people!" But it's almost like people floating around in the air. The first time I had one of these I really questioned what was going on, but it's now happened several times. It's almost like I'm peering into another dimension, and it's pretty spooky when it happens. They occur more often at night, and it might be something like walking into the house and seeing a lamp shade that looks exactly like a human head. A couple of times it looked like a complete human figure.

I've given half a dozen or more motivational speeches since my diagnosis and I always try to keep it light. I'm fully aware that the experts say there is no cure for the disease, and that it's progressive, and that I will get worse. But I also feel that my best chance for survival is to totally reject that prognosis and keep a 100 percent positive attitude about it. I also believe that good nutrition and rigid exercise will dramatically help my condition. When I give talks I don't say the "P" word, or dwell on the disease, but I do explain that I have this fashionable illness that's very in vogue, and that Michael J. Fox and Muhammad Ali have the same thing. I call it the "disease of the year." But then I talk about setting goals and writing them down, and never letting obstacles and unexplained events get in the way of those goals.

A Reluctant Astronaut

Shortly after I got the diagnosis I started reading everything I could about the disease, and the potential cures, while I do think the researchers are gaining ground on finding some answers, there's a long way to go. In August 2001, I joined an experimental group of people in Las Vegas who were participating in a clinical trial out of Yale University, to try to find some answers about Parkinson's. It was like being an astronaut and venturing up there into the unknown. It had been determined that there was a medicine that improved rats with Parkinson's and so some of us took the medicine and some were given a placebo. Of course I didn't know it at the time, but

I had the placebo. Eventually, the study ran out of money, but I'm glad I participated in it. It was an attempt to get involved in something that could have helped other patients and myself.

There are still about five publications that I read all the time to keep abreast of current developments. But I have skepticism about a lot that I read because the experts have screwed up so many times in their attempts to isolate a cure. One month they'll think they have the answers, and then they don't. So I focus on practical things I can do, like talking to people who have it and counseling people who may be struggling with it, especially the rookies who just got the news. I know that was the most difficult time for me and the most important time for me to speak to any person who could give me hope.

I have started doing some lobbying here and in Arizona as well. I can't remember the exact amount, but the government spends very little on research for Parkinson's cures; it's something like $4 per person, and that certainly needs to be increased. There also needs to be millions of dollars put into counseling and informing patients about the disease. It's clear from research I've done at the local level that the two national organizations involved in the disease have only identified about three to five percent of the sufferers. I know that whenever I talk to a fellow "Parkie," I learn as much or more about the disease as when I speak with doctors and researchers. So that fact alone cries out for more networking among those with the disease.

One of the things that bugs me about the research that has been done is that nobody has answered the big question yet: why do people get Parkinson's? I mean I've been diagnosed for four plus years now and I don't have a clue how I acquired this disease. Dr. Abraham Lieberman is considered the world's No. 1 expert on Parkinson's. He has said it could be related to toxicity issues. Well, I grew up in Las Vegas and was here in the early 50s when those mushroom clouds were being exploded at the Atomic Test

Site, so maybe there's a part of me glowing right now. But then why aren't tens of thousands of others afflicted who were exposed to the same elements? And there are rumblings that it's stress related, but I don't feel like I experience more stress than the average person. In fact, I think I'm known as being pretty easy going. Granted I got intense during the years that my business was growing, and I've always been pretty driven, but I can't believe that's the cause.

I do know that I would like to make a major contribution to finding some answers and easing the pain for people with Parkinson's. This disease is debilitating and difficult. It is not an easy thing, so I want to do something big as a response; maybe it could be funding research, or testifying in Washington D.C., or lobbying or fund-raising. In the early organizational meetings we've held in Las Vegas, we've already received pledges of $250,000 over the next five years. That's a pretty good start.

The Symptoms

Probably the worst single symptom of Parkinson's is fatigue. It seems like your body always feels like it's working overtime or being pushed to the limit. There are times when my arm weighs three times more than it should, so just lifting my arm from the table requires that much more energy. And the legs don't work the way they should when I walk. It's the old man shuffle. And the upper body stoops. I'm constantly trying to work on my posture and stand more upright. I exercise and do things to counteract the effects, like doing Pilates to build up the hamstrings, and I play tennis once a week in a doubles game and my partner and I still win our share. I know others with Parkinson's who stumble and even fall occasionally, but I haven't fallen yet. And the mind does not work as fast. Words are more difficult to come by and the speech can get slurred, especially in the afternoon, around 2 o'clock, when I really start to get tired. Actually working on this manuscript is exhausting, because I'm always struggling to find the right word, or the perfect anecdote, to make everything come alive. And there are times when I can't read my own writing because one of the common symptoms of the disease is Micrographia, whereby the handwriting becomes much smaller and more compact. Thank God Jack Sheehan is a verbose Irishman who has a way of reading my mind and finding the words that don't come easily to me. Together, we seem to find a way to deliver the message.

I try to take naps about two each afternoon, but I'm not very good at it. I have a couch in my office, and I know I need more naps, but my mind doesn't shut down the way I wish it would so the naps could be more restful and refreshing. I probably sleep about 4 1/2 to 5 1/2 hours a night, and I then I wake up and can't go back to sleep. So I'll read a book. The doctors tell me I need more rest or I'll be in trouble, so I need to work on that. But you are who you are. Last year I took my secretary Barb and my associate Monte from the office to Europe, and they will attest to the fact that I ran them ragged all over the continent. It's just not in my nature to remain passive and sit still for too long.

Oh, before I forget, there's one other "delicious" little symptom with Parkinson's. If you're not careful you drool. I just have to make sure I don't do that when I'm staring at a pretty woman. Sherry might get upset.

Chapter 5

The Gift

Not only does Bruce bring out the best in you, but he initiates a process of making you want to spread this good will to others. He generates a chain reaction of virtue and positive energy. — Diane Layne

My friends and family members say that I have a "gift." People immediately *trust* me. I connect with them, and I have an ability to motivate them to *care*, to take action, to get more involved in causes and improve the world they inhabit.

I believe that this gift that people talk about was genetically passed on to me from my grandmother on my mother's side, Grandma Mimi. As you'll learn, she was an amazing woman, years ahead of her time, and she had a terrific impact on me as a young man growing up with some difficult family challenges, and even later on when I was building my business. She always told me I could do anything I wanted to do in life. Having an adult give you the assurance that

you can reach for the moon and touch it is invaluable. I have always told my sons the same thing, and will also impart that affirmation to my beautiful grandchildren.

Grandma Mimi had a great way with people, always making them feel good about themselves and treating them with openness and sincerity, so I think she deserves a lot of credit for her inspiration.

To a certain extent, my ability to analyze people and situations was developed partly through my formal education and my studies in economics. I learned how to dissect abstracts and how to arrive at logical conclusions. If you asked my editor Jack about my abstract

Mimi

35

thinking, he would probably tell you I do it to a fault. He says I employ far too many abstract nouns in my retelling of stories, and he has turned me into a stickler for anecdotes, those revealing little stories that tell so much about a person. I guess Jack would tell you that "abstract" thinking has its limitations, but it has certainly helped me in addressing business challenges and solving problems.

In my business it has helped to work with people at the top of organizations, and I have had a knack for befriending the No. 1 person in the company, whether it's the National Parkinson's Disease Foundation or the president of Mandalay Bay. I feel that, if I can share my vision with the top person and listen to his or her concerns, we will always stay on the same page in our business relationship, and things will run smoothly.

A Gift of Caring

If I were to define my gift, it would embrace a lot of different traits: enthusiasm, a total openness, and a sixth sense that allows me to feel people's pain and to truly want to listen to their problems and concerns and help them find a solution. I've read a lot of positive literature and self-improvement books; I know that problems are not solved by accident, and you don't work your way out of tough situations by waiting for a lucky break. You must look for answers and be open to solutions. One example is the Pilates program I'm on with Dr. Keith Kleven. I had read that by strengthening the abdomen and stomach and working on the core muscles of the body, I could slow down some of the debilitating effects of Parkinson's. Gracie is my personal trainer, and she does a great job pushing me to my limit each time. I'm sharing the lessons and drills I've learned from her with the national Parkinson's people, because I know thousands could benefit from these exercises. There's no question that my walk and my posture have improved since doing Pilates.

Grandma Mimi

I'm always giving away copies of books I find inspirational so that people can find their own answers, but it's typical of most people that they have to be pushed by someone to find the right direction. I enjoy the role of motivator, and I think people sense that. One of the best feelings I've ever had is knowing I helped someone out of a jam, and I can't think of a greater "Thank You" than when young people come up to me at restaurants or sporting events and say that they heard me speak to their class and that I made a difference in their life.

I think this ability to motivate people is a major reason that Layne & Associates became the largest private insurance broker in the state. I was able to get employees to buy in immediately to our philosophy of customer service, and they knew that if they performed well that I would be behind them a thousand percent. That's what great teamwork is all about, people pulling together behind a leader with vision.

I also have a sense about how things will turn out if I follow a particular path. I have a certainty that if I push the right buttons people will react in an appropriate way. I don't know where this comes from; maybe it's God-given or maybe it's inspired by all the stuff I read. I'm not sure. But I do know it involves showing people that you really care about their problem and that you are willing to listen carefully and try to help them work through it. I guess if I hadn't been inspired to pursue the insurance business I might have gone into some sort of counseling. It's satisfying that I could do both at the same time.

I've always been curious about the components of leadership and what makes some people leaders and others followers. Why did people follow Hitler, or James Jones in Jonestown, or David Koresh in Waco, Texas? What power does Osama Bin Laden have? These were men who led people to do evil or self-destruct. So I guess these men had the power to find weakness in people and take advantage of it. They used the gift negatively.

On a dogsled team, if you are just a follower, and not a leader, the scenery never changes. — BL

Positive Leadership Traits

Loyalty: This is number one on my list of traits that I look for in employees. It is the measure of how much one wants to excel in life. I like to think I was an excellent role model for our employees because I worked 60 hours a week and took great pride in our company's professionalism and reputation. I wanted the company to be always in pursuit of excellence, and I think that inspired our employees to work extra hard. Through my example, they'd often come in and work on weekends and do what it took to succeed. I am just a real sucker for loyalty and for somebody who works hard in the clutch. Those people are dear to me and I always make sure I take care of them. Once they see that loyalty is rewarded, it becomes ingrained in their work habits.

I learn from the great leaders through history. People would have followed Napoleon off a cliff, and although conventional wisdom was that the earth was square, loyal followers signed on with Christopher Columbus and believed his theory that the earth was round. They staked their lives on their belief in him.

When I think of loyalty at Layne & Associates I think of Monte Smith, who has been with me for over 25 years. If you think back a quarter century ago, it was not exactly a great arena for women in business. When Monte was hired, she started out as a part-time receptionist; she now is in charge of the entire Mandalay Bay account, which is a multi-million-dollar annual account. Bill Wright has been my loyal friend and confidant for over 14 years, a true "right-hand man." He's a gifted speech writer, and I hope that he knows how deeply I appreciate him. And I think about my secretary Barbara Saccamano, who has been with me for almost 10 years. She works extra hours and takes work home with her and is totally loyal.

And I can't think about loyalty without feeling gratitude for the many wonderful clients who helped Layne & Associates grow through the years. For instance there was Las Vegas Paving, owned by Bob Mendenhall, the most creative guy I've ever met. He has 65 federal patents, including an asphalt recycling machine that saves untold taxpayer dollars. They've been with us for almost 20 years. And MJ DiBiase Construction, the largest painting and drywall contractor in the state of Nevada, and their owners Susan and Sherman Simmons, who have been with us for 25 years. And of course Mandalay Bay Resort and Mike Ensign and Dave Belding, who even though they had a large claim still kept their insurance with us and were totally cooperative in helping us make the sale to Brown and Brown. You just can't put a value on the importance of that kind of loyalty.

Enthusiasm comes with caring. I know that "caring" is a hokey word, and hard to define. But it's being interested and passionate about something, and it is the characteristic that made Layne & Associates successful. You know enthusiasm exists immediately upon meeting someone. When I would interview a person for a job, I could usually tell within 10 minutes whether he or she had the qualities I was looking for. Body language is extremely important. But it's not everything. There are some people that do well in interviews because they've had so many different jobs and they have had a lot of practice interviewing. So you can be fooled.

From everything I've seen, Bruce Layne is the real deal, and there aren't a whole lot of people you can say that about.
— Curt Anderson

Being a Mentor: I've been a coach several times for kids' athletic teams and have spoken repeatedly to high school and college students on career days. I would estimate that I have spoken to over 4,000 kids on the ingredients of success. I always ask them whether they want to make a lot of money, and if they do I tell them they have to be in the sales end of a business. I talk to them about setting up their goals, and I make them commit to goals in the classroom. I explain the importance of writing down those goals because it makes them more accountable. I have done this for seniors in high school on Career Day, and I have also done it at UNLV for 25 years. I do not think there's anything that I take more pride in than inspiring kids and knowing I made a difference in their lives at a critical juncture.

I will ask kids, "What is your objective in life?" And I ask them to give me their definitions of success. One kid told me it was owning a Porsche. He obviously did not get it. And then there are the idealists who want to save the world.

Having Fun: It's always important to me to incorporate fun into any project, and that brings me to a story about when I was coaching my sons' Little League teams. When I was coaching baseball with the kids it was my belief that when they're little you let every kid play and move them around to different positions in the infield and outfield so they can experience the whole game and the strategies involved at the various positions. I think our record was 15 wins and 1 loss at the time and I made a substitution at pitcher, and the other team started pounding away at the guy I brought in. Although we were ahead something like 10 to 4 in the last inning, we ended up losing the game. And this woman who was a cocktail waitress at Caesars Palace had a boy on the team — I remember she was always late to pick him up, and I would often have to wait with him for 45 minutes after everyone else left until his mother arrived — and, of course, she complained to the league officials about my coaching after we lost that game. The commissioner of the league was John Spilotro, whose brother Tony Spilotro was a known mob guy whose character was played by Joe Pesci in the movie *Casino*. Tony, as we all know, ended up tortured and murdered with another brother. They were buried alive in a cornfield in Indiana. Anyway, John Spilotro calls me and basically suggests I rethink my coaching methods, because there had been some complaints. He said there had been a couple parents that were upset. Anyway, the net result is that they drove a good man out of coaching. I guess the moral of that story is that the parents often can be worse than the kids, and that when something quits having any element of fun in it, it's time to do something else.

Respect for Others: I got a good lesson one day in what has become known around the office as "the Carlotta story." Carlotta was this sweet little lady, probably in her late 50s at the time, and a veteran in the insurance business. She was rather eccentric, a short, clubby little thing with dark hair, who worked as a customer service rep. She would come in and most days put on her bedroom slippers because her feet hurt. Well, in the days when we were buying computers and putting them at everyone's desk, they were coming in just one or two at a time and we had sort of a pecking order on who got them first, based on seniority. And someone who had been with us a shorter period of time than Carlotta got a computer before she did. Carlotta leaned over my desk and said, "I have some seniority here and I should have gotten my computer last week. I want it now!" She was pretty fired up about it. And I told her, "Carlotta, it is tough to decide what to do with these computers and I know that nobody is happy. I'm having a tough time disbursing them. You have to understand it's kind of lonely at the top."

And she leaned even further over my desk and said, "Well, it's lonely at the bottom, too!"

That was an all-time great line. I made sure she got her computer that day, damn it!

Staying Focused: When it comes to business decisions, it's critical to stay focused and not let emotion get the better of you. Maintaining dignity in a heated battle is important. A recent example was this Mandalay Bay situation where there was pending litigation over the ground sinking when it was under construction. I could not sell Layne & Associates to a larger firm with the litigation hanging over our head, and I had been told four different times that we would not be sued in the end, and four times the people at Mandalay Bay came back to us and said they were sorry but they had to keep us in the litigation. But I remained calm through that whole period of time, which was well over a year. In the end, they put a cap on our liability and that made it possible for the deal to go through. They turned out to be people of their word, but I think the fact that I remained unflappable and kept a lid on the situation allowed for a good resolution.

Reliability: I think I missed something like two days of work in 25 years. That doesn't go unnoticed by other employees, and I think that's why we've had such good performance through the years. In our heyday, we rarely lost accounts, probably only one or two accounts in 10 or 15 years, and most places don't hold accounts for that length of time.

Perseverance: You have to be resourceful in life and hang in there regardless of the circumstances. When I got the opportunity to work for Marsh and McLennan early in my career, they were the world's largest insurance broker. I was making $550 a month, but it was a start. It felt better than when I was working at the titanium plant, going nowhere, and feeling scared to death I was going to end up a big zero.

Later on, it was difficult having to study to get that masters degree in insurance, what with being married with two little kids. That was 25 hours per week extra that I really didn't have. And much later it took perseverance to form the Southern Nevada Clean Communities committee. It was difficult because I had to raise $50,000 to start the program and serve as its president for the first three years. But I did not give up on it, even though there were a lot of obstacles. Community beautification was not everyone's top priority, and yet it was an important service that needed to be done.

Through the years at Layne & Associates I always had that gnawing fear that we could go out of business. That never really went away completely until we made the deal with Brown and Brown. So there was an element of perseverance in working hard month after month, year after year to make it grow and stave off those fears or extinction.

And certainly the battle against Parkinson's requires perseverance. Driving to the workout place to do Pilates twice a week to strengthen my stomach muscles and abdomen is not easy, and yet it's helped my posture and my gait tremendously. Playing tennis helps as well. It's not quite the recreation it would be were I totally healthy, but it's something I need to continue to do.

Self-Discipline: is a first cousin of perseverance. It takes self-discipline to stay on an exercise regimen, and to do the things necessary to become a better and more effective person. I started in Toastmasters because I didn't believe I had a very good education in communications. There were 10 of us who met at 7:30 in the morning to practice public speaking and make presentations. As a result, I became a much more effective public speaker than I'd been before. I still have a ways to go — and my lack of public speaking expertise was just Reason No. 483 of the five hundred reasons I wasn't elected lieutenant governor — but at least I'm working on it.

Finding Business Strategies that Work: I learned early on that, rather than use the old axiom about treating the customer's needs first, it made more sense to look at the employees' needs first and know that if employees are treated right they will pass that treatment on to the customers. We also hear a lot about a company staying lean and cutting the fat to reduce overhead. Well, what worked for me was what we'll call "keeping it fat." If I found a good person with a lot of ability, I would create a position for that person and know that in the process I'd be improving the entire operation. Dennis Stein is an example of that. He used to run Citicorp when it had 1,600 employees. When he joined us we had 40, and then the number grew to 80. One area where this didn't work was in sales. I always tried to hire people from different industries to be salespeople, but it never worked out. If they could sell, they could sell. If they couldn't, they couldn't.

I also came up with a better and cheaper way for hotels to buy liability insurance. I was always looking for an analytical way for hotels to solve their insurance problems because their premiums were always going up, doubling and tripling every year, and the only way to control the claims was that the hotels had to have better investigation reports. So I came up with a specialized investigation form that security guards could fill out. They would just have to check mark certain things so there was some authentication to what happened with an incident. Where was the spilled liquid? Where was the banana peel you slipped on? So the investigation system had to be improved, and secondly, it was important to settle the claim quickly. The quicker it's settled the cheaper it is because if it drags on the people go back to Iowa and they have a friend who has a friend who got $52,000 for the same kind of slip-and-fall and whiplash.

Adjusting an insurance claim is a real art, and at its core it's about dealing with people. In the end most people just want a hug and they want you to say you're sorry. All of those Del Webb Hotels we represented had claims, and some that I thought would be for $10,000 or $25,000 we were able to settle for a buffet pass and a couple of cocktails. We just had better internal controls and were able to utilize an internal claims coordinator so we could stay on top of the information before too much time passed and memories faded. We actually used to have seminars for security guards and give them pride in filling out the reports.

A Sense of Humor: This is so important in the overall scheme of things. I don't consider myself a funny person, but I'm generally in a cheerful or sunny mood. If you ask people they'll tell you I'm never in a bad mood. Even when I got the news about Parkinson's, I snapped out of it very quickly (although I did have Sherry remove all the razor blades from the house). I had about four really bad days. Today I might have the occasional insecurity attack, or feel a sense of inadequacy, but I don't let it make me dour or unpleasant. Despite how much competitiveness exists in a workplace, underlying it all there has to be a lightheartedness that makes the workplace pleasant. If it's too stressful, people will quit and you won't maintain loyalty.

To be a positive leader, you have to find the good in people and help them overcome a weakness or solve a problem that fate tosses in their path. And I just love the challenge of doing that. I consider it a blessing that people are more than willing to share with me. It is truly *My Gift*.

Bruce & Sherry Halloween, 1985 (above). Bruce and Sherry, fund raising for Southern Nevada's clean up (left).

(*Editor's note: Two others close to Bruce, his long-time business associate Monte Smith and his daughter-in-law Diane Layne, both appreciate Bruce's "gift" and chose to offer descriptions of it.*)

Monte and Bruce

Monte Smith

I was tickled when I heard that Bruce's book was going to be labeled The Gift, *because it is the perfect title for his life story.*

It's not easy defining this gift that Bruce possesses, but it becomes instantly evident to anyone who meets him. He has this uncanny ability to form an instant rapport with people and make them as comfortable as an old bedroom slipper. He has referred to it as the "wounded puppy dog" appeal, but it's much more than that. He has this way of bringing out the best in people and actually getting them to hold their heads higher and feel better about their place in the world.

His gift is equal parts contagious enthusiasm and positive attitude, plus a kind heart and easily identifiable integrity. There are some people

41

who look you dead in the eye and try to form an instant connection, but it's almost like they learned the trick in a textbook. You never quite buy the brand of sincerity they're trying to sell. But Bruce is just the opposite. People sense instantly that what they see is what they get with him, and it's amazing how within the first hour so many people confide in him with information they haven't shared with those they've known for years. Maybe he should have been a priest listening to confessions. He would have gotten an earful.

But it's even more than that, because the reason people young and old share things with him is because they trust that he will offer good advice. That is why he is such a good mentor to young people and fellow workers who need a shoulder to lean on. They just sense instantly that he has a good heart and will give them counsel that is sincere and well informed. With too many people who are quick with advice, the listener feels like he's being lectured to, or spoken down to. With Bruce, you always have the feeling that his response has no ulterior motive, but rather that his primary concern is giving helpful information or a carefully thought out opinion. That is why he has been such a great boss for these last 26 years, and more than that, a great friend.

Diane Layne

Bruce Layne is one of those phenomenal, rare people that make you feel that life and humanity are truly wonderful and that you should stop and recognize their great beauty. I know this because not only have I adopted Bruce as my father, but I consider him a great mentor. Bruce rejuvenates my ability to savor life on a regular basis. All I have to do is talk to him for 30 seconds. "Thirty seconds" is a standing joke between us because he is very busy living life to the fullest, but he always makes sure that he takes time, even if it's just 30 seconds, to call or visit. Joking aside, that is part of his gift: to always be willing to take the time to share his wisdom, kindness, and positive outlook with friends, family, and even strangers.

Bruce is continually making himself more interesting by experiencing every bit of life that he can. He reads everything. He travels the world. He exercises on a regular basis, takes classes, plays the guitar, has a demanding profession, and is very involved in the community, to name just a few of his activities.

Bruce thrives on helping people and taking a sincere interest in their lives. As you speak to him you find yourself feeling important and special. People are comfortable opening up and not speaking through a shield that we all seem to hide behind. Bruce has the ability to bring back that freeness and candor that you have as a child before you build up barriers from life's harsh realities. He doesn't intentionally set out to break down barriers, but as you speak to him he just naturally brings out the best in you. For example, as I am writing about him and his gift it is motivating me to be a better person for myself as well as for others. I feel like spending more quality time with my children or maybe writing more or giving to a charity. Not only does Bruce bring out the best in you, he initiates a process of making you want to spread this good will to others. He is a man who has a grand purpose on this earth, and anyone who comes in contact with him will benefit from his gift.

I truly believe that the sparkle that comes from within my son Garrett Bruce is, in fact, the very same gift that his grandfather radiates.

Chapter 6
What I've Learned
A Letter to Maddie and Garrett Bruce and Anyone Else Who'd Like to Listen

might wonder whether a nun would be the best source of ways to have fun, but it's a very clever and insightful book. Some of her suggestions are to "live alone for a while," and to "find a place to escape reality." She also has a chapter called "think about nuns." That one makes me smile. Actually, the whole book makes me smile.

Other bits of wisdom in the book:

— "Anyone who is funny knows that there is a dear price to be paid for all the foolishness."

— "Having more fun than anyone else means you also have to work twice as hard at everything for not being serious enough, and you are most likely to be taken less seriously as a result."

— "Nothing refreshes, comforts, and heals like a good time."

— "Nothing exhilarates and sends the soul soaring more than having the best time ever, so much so that face muscles ache from such heavy laughter. You must know that kind of fun often before you die."

I've always been a voracious reader of inspirational materials, any books and articles that would help me find my way or offer new insights on living. And I've always felt an inherent eagerness to pass the collective wisdom of smart people on to others. There's a book that I've given to about 25 people called *Ten Fun Things to Do Before You Die*, by a nun named Karol Jackowski. One

I think you understood this last one when you were very little, Maddie. On your first birthday, people gave you lots of beautiful stuffed animals and toys. My present to you was a rubber chicken that I had gotten from an Area 51 promotion. You loved that chicken, and would dig it out

43

from all the other toys in your toy box. And on your second birthday, I gave you a beach ball from the Nevada Realty advertising campaign. You enjoyed it as much as any other present that year. You "get it": the thought is much more important than the present.

Maddie and rubber chicken, her first birthday gift from Bruce

Through my life I've tried to live by certain principles, and by doing so I've found more than my share of happiness and contentment. I'm sure all of us would respond to the question: "Do you want to be happy and content in your life?" with the answer, "Of course I would!" Yet how many of us really work at that goal, and write down certain pearls of wisdom that we can reread over and over again and instill in our daily living?

I'm a great believer in the notion that we must establish a personal program for spirituality and set up a pro-active program for happiness. That means establishing

44

some principles and writing them down and focusing on them on a daily basis. You really need to think about your prescription for happiness to make it happen, and then exercise it every day the same way you would a muscle.

Here's a short list of the **principles I try to live by**:

- ❀ Have a list of principles that you write down and refer to constantly.
- ❀ Have more fun than anyone else.
- ❀ Have more tolerance and patience.
- ❀ Have a higher level of acceptance.
- ❀ Experience more joy in life.
- ❀ Instill in yourself optimism as a way of life.
- ❀ Find pockets of fulfillment.
- ❀ Focus on the present.

The Importance of Compassion

I see in Bruce a true friend, a person who stepped forward when he did not have to, who took on my problems as if they were as important as his own, who looked after me when I was at the bottom. He is a real 'doctor of the spirit.'
— *Susan DiBiase Simmons*

I have been told many times that I am a compassionate person. What this usually means is that people who make that comment to me find me more compassionate than themselves. If someone were more compassionate than I, he or she probably wouldn't make that observation. But it's true that I do want to help people who have problems, and I feel genuine empathy for someone going through a difficult challenge. Just like the cowboys who wore the white hats on Saturday mornings, I feel bad for the less fortunate or the underdog. I've always felt bad about the fact that we have homeless people in this country. And I feel bad for the African nations that are starving. Who is more noble than Mother Theresa or Gandhi, individuals who gave up all their creature comforts to help those less fortunate?

I never liked firing anyone, even if the person richly deserved to be fired. And I've always taken a great satisfaction from being able to help anyone, from friends and business associates to students that might need some inspiration or assistance.

While I'm not one that particularly cares for the "I'm a victim" cop-out that we hear so often in our society, I genuinely do care about people and I feel their pain. And remember, this is all coming from an insurance salesman. (Maybe you need to rethink your opinion of our profession.)

Growing up, I lived in a bad section of Las Vegas, at 8th and Carson, which was downtown Las Vegas. Right across the street from us was the Unemployment Office, and there were always 10 to 15 shabbily dressed men there looking for a job or waiting outside for someone to pick them up to go to work. That made an impression on me, and I always felt sorry for them.

This compassion I feel has been reflected in the way I've treated employees over my 30 years in business. I've given them money when they were in need, offered direction when they requested it, and have even helped some with the American Dream of buying a house. I even participated in an intervention with one employee, when his mother requested my help, by going to his house and taking him to Charter Hospital to overcome a dependency problem.

I've always felt that it was my responsibility as a person who hires people to help those employees become better people. I want the person who comes through our door the first time to leave a much better person and feel that our company helped him or her grow in every way. I've hired a lot of people that didn't have extensive résumés, but I believed in them as people. They often are more productive than the person with the glitzy résumé because they are so grateful for being given a better opportunity.

The reason I've done these things is very simple: I care, and these gestures are extremely important, both to the person I can help and to myself. It gives me a feeling that my life has purpose.

It's important to remember that compassion should not only be felt towards others, but also toward ourselves. I'm not sure who said it, but a good message is that we need to learn to be aware of our own accomplishments, to have compassion for ourselves, and to praise our own achievements — all things we probably give to others without a moment's hesitation.

Tim, Mimi, Bruce, Frank Layne

Achieving Balance

I've also learned that the daily grind of life and all the sad occurrences that we inevitably are confronted with can be balanced somewhat if we surround ourselves with fun people. We do have a choice about whom we spend our time with, and I make an effort to choose friends and companions that are fun to be around. Lord knows there are far too few of these fun people around to fill our days and nights, and seemingly fewer survive adulthood. I also think friends should be people with depth, who have insight and are interesting and challenging in conversation. There are tons of people who are a mile wide and an inch deep. Why not choose friends that are a mile deep?

I know it's not true that the older you get, the less there is to make you laugh. On the contrary, the older I get the more there is that makes me laugh, and the less there is that bugs me or throws me for a loop. It's a fine art to have a great time when alone, but the pure joy of all that fun gets divinely multiplied and intensified by the company of other people. It's an amazing grace that the time capsule in my mind is loaded with precious memories of fun times, any of which can get me laughing just as hard today as it did when the event occurred. Reflecting on those moments can also help pull you out of a dark mood when gremlins start creeping into your thoughts. I'm proud of the fact that I have learned how to push away depression when too much reflection on my "Parkie" status starts to bring me down.

In seeking out fun people to be around, here are some things to watch for: ❀ a good appetite, ❀ interesting work, ❀ an ability to tell a good story, ❀ a slightly twisted sense of humor, ❀ fresh insights, ❀ brave choices.

The more of these attributes or character traits a person has, the more fun he or she is to be around and the more laughter they will generate.

Dr. Jack Jurasky, a Las Vegas psychiatrist and friend, likes to say that our everyday existence relies on various stages of survival. We are surviving from one day to the next, and sometimes the circumstances become extreme, but to really enhance the quality of life a person needs to experience what Jurasky calls "finding HELL on earth." It sounds daunting, but it means exactly the opposite of what it implies:

Happiness (meaning gratification). You can find happiness by finding gratifying things to do. Think what you ideally would want to do in life, and then do it and enjoy it.

Enthusiasm, have a great curiosity about things and then pursue them.

Love. It can be defined by seeing beauty in a kiwi or in a sunrise. The analogy that Jurasky shared with Jack Sheehan about the monk appreciating the beauty of a buttercup growing out of a limb that he's clinging to as he's falling to his death is certainly appropriate to a definition of love.

Laughter. It comes naturally by finding the humor in life, by keeping things in perspective, and by looking for it. The more you seek out laughter and amusement the more you'll be able to find it. Laughter is difficult to find in a dark cave.

By looking for hell on earth, we find a sense of commonality among all living creatures and gain a greater appreciation for our universe. A wise man once said that fear of insignificance is the biggest fear of most men, and there's truth in that. Is there any more hollow feeling than leaving this earth with the notion that we didn't make a difference at all, or have any positive impact on another's life? Writing this book has taken away my fear of death, because I know that I've done good things.

Philosophy of Life

The more purpose you have, the easier life will be. You have to have a purpose, and put it in writing. My personal purpose is to grow and learn, and universal purpose is to make a significant contribution, somewhere, somehow. Having a purpose will help you handle and appreciate life.

I'm a wisdom junkie of sorts. I'll dog-ear books or articles that contain ideas I think are valuable, and I'll often photo-copy them and give them to friends or people in the office. Wisdom is meant to be shared with others, so hopefully we can all get a little smarter in the way we conduct our lives. Here are several ideas or snippets of knowledge that I think have great validity:

The most important thing we do in life is pursue our spiritual quest. Obviously, the more meaning we give to our lives the greater will be our purpose for living.

Your life should be lived with the guiding determination to make a significant contribution to yourself and to the rest of humanity. This will help you appreciate life more, and you will find peace and contentment, satisfaction and fulfillment.

We are all trying to find the road to contentment. I have found six fundamentals that help me find that contentment. I try to review them and practice them every day and incorporate them totally into my life.

1. **Faith**: It's the source of everything significant in our lives. Inspiration, positive action, and conscience are all connected to faith, which some might call a blind trust. Faith is a firm belief without solid evidence. Spiritual faith is trusting God, and seeing Her as a benevolent being. One of my daily affirmations is that with a sincere faith in God and myself, I will have the confidence, courage, and conviction to go about my daily life and accept the bad and the good. I believe that healing depends on faith. It is my faith that convinces me a cure will be found for Parkinson's in my lifetime. And it is my faith that gives me the positive attitude to battle this thing all the way. From my Catholic religion, I've learned the importance of prayer and how it can have a calming effect in times of stress. I do believe the theology of the Church is sound and enduring and hopefully the Catholic religion can survive through all the tragedies of abusive priests and the cover-ups that took place to hide this shameful behavior from the public.

2. **Tolerance and Patience from pain and suffering**: The Dalai Lama writes about this in *The Art of Happiness*. He has a set of beliefs that function as substrata for all of his actions: a belief in the fundamental gentleness and goodness of human beings, a belief in the value of compassion, a belief in a policy of kindness, and a sense of commonality among all living creatures. He says we must train our mind, and that can lead to a transformation of our entire attitude. The Dalai Lama says we must eliminate those factors that lead to suffering and cultivate those that lead to happiness. This can be manifested in a simple willingness to reach out to others to create a feeling of infinity and good will.

3. **Happiness**: Both the Dalai Lama and Rabbi Kushner have said that happiness is an emotion that comes on a moment-to-moment basis. As much as we'd like happiness to be a permanent condition, it doesn't work that way. But it's important to appreciate that happiness is determined more by one's state of mind than by external events. Happiness certainly isn't derived from material things. Witness the beatific expression of contentment that never left the face of Mother Teresa, who lived in utter poverty but was uplifted by the great feeling of knowing that she was helping others; and the look of discontent that exists

on the faces of many very wealthy people who are miserable because they are consumed by greed and money. I can honestly say that Parkinson's disease has in many positive ways transformed my life. I appreciate much more just waking up in the morning and seeing what the day will bring. True happiness comes not from merely having what we want, but from appreciating what we have.

4. **Inspiration**: It is all around us if our eyes are open to it. I gain inspiration from Christopher Reeve, who rather than wasting time on self-pity has chosen to use his mind and his celebrity to increase awareness and to educate the public about spinal cord injuries. His infinite determination to walk again and his unwavering conviction that it will happen serve as inspiration to thousands of people who have suffered similar injuries. His faith is absolutely unwavering. I'm also inspired by the fact that he hasn't given up his occupation of writing and directing films.

5. *The Power of Now*: Eckhart Toole wrote a book called *The Power of Now,* which is a guide to spiritual enlightenment. The essence of the book is that "now" is all-important and that living in the present is much healthier than dwelling in the past or worrying about the future. I know that great golfers like Tiger Woods emphasize the importance of playing the sport "in the present tense." The typical weekend golfer like myself tends to fret over bad shots and let them affect the next ones. Tiger has learned, probably through the influence of his Asian mother and her belief in Eastern philosophy, how to block out the previous five minutes and the five minutes to come and give his full attention to the shot he's hitting at the moment.

Toole's book talks about wonderful healings and transformations and how to increase the level of joy in your life. He says it's our own mind that generates much of our pain and problems, not other people or outside influences, and that if we can channel our own thoughts toward contentment and living in the "now," we will keep our mind more quiet and content. I highly recommend this book to everyone.

6. **Positive Self-Talk, or Learned Optimism**: When something bad happens, pessimists perceive it as permanent. Optimists perceive it as temporary.

Finally, a short list of watchwords that I use myself, and encourage others to use in a search for a better life:

Have a clearly defined sense of purpose for your life that you write down and refer to daily.

Integrate into that sense of purpose your faith, and make certain that your life goals always stay in harmony with your larger beliefs.

Build a philosophy of life based on common sense and your everyday experiences, and live by it.

Keep a positive self-image. You will be far more attractive to others and set your own bar higher if you don't get down on yourself or diminish your self-importance.

Search for 10s in your life, those moments that you will celebrate with your friends and loved ones and cherish forever.

Hone your talents constantly. Acknowledge your gifts and areas in which you excel, and work at being even better at them.

Endeavor to create satisfaction and contentment wherever you go. Leave people smiling, not frowning.

Savor the richness of life and never take the wonderful people and moments you share with them for granted.

Always remain in the pursuit of happiness.

I am convinced that, if you follow these guidelines, you not only will find more happiness and fulfillment in your life, but you will inspire others to do the same. You will, in fact, Pay it Forward.

Chapter 7

In the Ring

Bruce was the first extremely business-oriented member we'd had on the Nevada Athletic Commission, and he dramatically increased our business credibility. — Marc Ratner

I was appointed to the Nevada State Athletic Commission by Governor Bob Miller in December of 1990. This body oversees all the boxing and wrestling matches that are approved by the state of Nevada, and nowadays that even includes those all-out wars they call Ultimate Fighting. It's pretty brutal stuff.

I was put on the Commission to lend more business expertise and so it could be run more efficiently. There were previous commissioners who were thought to be too close to promoters like Don King and Bob Arum, and so my function really was to bring more credibility and stability to the commission. It's funny because it is thought to be such a highly coveted position, and yet from a monetary standpoint it's worthless.

We made $80 a month and put in countless hours. Prior to my being named to the Commission, there was a lot of world travel involved, flying to places like Thailand, to make sure the matches that were approved were legit. But the budget was tightened by the time I was on it, so the traveling was cut way back and there wasn't that much glamour to it. Our most important challenge was to make certain that the matches arranged by promoters were not mismatches. Don King would find these guys out in the hinterlands who would have records of 28 and zero, but they hadn't fought anybody, and if you weren't careful you could have a totally lopsided fight. The number one priority was to make certain we never had a death in the ring because of a mismatch.

Everyone who's been in Las Vegas for any length of time remembers Duk Koo Kim dying in the fight with Boom Boom Mancini. That was just a tragedy, perhaps a case of a referee's not stopping a fight soon enough. A fight is supposed to be stopped when a boxer is in serious trouble and is not fighting back, or when he is rendered defenseless. That is a real art, knowing when to stop a fight and when to let the boxers continue. And it is the Commission's responsibility to make certain we have the best-trained referees possible.

Bringing Business Sense to Boxing

I think I brought the Commission up to speed as far as being business-like. When I joined it, there was only a one-page form for promoters, and we could not even get to their bank accounts to see that the funds were there. I got the Gaming Control Board's 50-page application and boiled it down to about six or seven pages. The new form also gave us the right to go to the bank and check accounts and statements.

The Commission is made up of five people, usually two from the northern part of the state and three from Southern Nevada, and there's always battles going on with that. On the Commission with me were Dr. Elias Ghanem; Dr. Jim Nave, who was really the stabilizing force and the most knowledgeable of us about boxing; Luther Mack from Reno; and Nat Carasali, who owns the Peppermill in Reno.

There was a lot of negative feedback initially when Miller appointed me because the naysayers said I was his crony and that I didn't know boxing. Even Royce Feour, who covers boxing for the *Las Vegas Review-Journal*, was critical, but after interviewing me he was turned around. He even penned a column with the headline "Layne Good Pick for Commission" shortly after I was named.

To be frank, I wasn't even a big boxing fan prior to being named to the Commission, but it turned out to be a very interesting experience. I've been to the Super Bowl, the NBA Playoffs, the World Series and other great sporting events, but nothing compares to a heavyweight boxing championship. That's the most electric sports event you can ever attend, and of course as a Commissioner I had front-row seats.

My wife is a former Junior League President and I thought she was the type that would not like these fights, yet she came to really enjoy them. The kids, of course, had a great time and they still talk about it. We used to have little parties for our clients at the agency prior to the fights, and we always made it a real outing.

I remember the night the Fan Man parachuted into the ring and interrupted the second Evander Holyfield-Riddick Bowe fight outdoors at Caesars Palace. I was sitting right next to Minister Louis Farrakhan of the Nation of Islam and Jesse Jackson, and Jackson got up and ran out of there. He thought that this guy who fell from the heavens was after him. Farrakhan just stared at the Fan Man as he was lying helpless in the ring, and his two bodyguards pistol-whipped the guy with their telephones. What the guy had done was kind of innovative, albeit stupid, but he got the crap beat out of him by these guys. They were thugs, really.

Staying Above the Fray

When you're on that Commission you're really dealing with the underbelly of society, meaning the fight promoters and the poor fighters from the streets with a different mentality. You find yourself getting protective with the underdogs. You don't want to see them get hurt or ripped off financially, and yet it happens all the time. We were in charge of everything: the judges, the referees, even making certain that they put the right number of wraps of tape on their hands before pulling on the gloves. But it's well known in the boxing world that we have the most level playing field here in Nevada. If you don't want a level playing field, you go to Texas or New York or wherever, because no one has a commission that is as stringent as ours. We may get a lot of negative remarks about us because we host the most big fights, but we have the best judges, the best refs, and the best fight doctors in the world.

And the money is huge for these fights. You have fighters getting $15 and $20 million for these bouts and the promoters trying to gyp them out of it. Promoters like Don King will do a contract with a fighter and then go to another state and change the contract and draw up another one that supersedes the first one. The Nevada rule is that, of the total purse that a fighter signs for, the manager of record can take no more than one third. Unfortunately, these sanctioning bodies that okay the fighters and rank the fighters are too much under the control of the promoters.

Promoters can arrange all sorts of side deals because they have so much power over the sport. For instance, Don King can arrange things because Jose Sulaiman, who is the president of the World Boxing Council, is King's best friend, so the rankings become very arbitrary. And Sulaiman holds the title of lifetime director of the WBC. It's like being the Pope or a Supreme Court Justice. He can't be replaced. And he controls who is ranked and in what position. In boxing it's a case of the rich getting richer and the powerful getting more powerful. What it comes down to is that you can't trust anybody around you in the boxing world. As a commissioner you just have to roll with your convictions and try to ignore the pressure that people put on you.

Don King called me shortly after I was named to the Commission and asked me to lunch. And I said I'd go, but that I would bring my office manager with me. He didn't like that, my bringing a witness to the conversation, so he broke the date and tried shortly thereafter to set up a dinner. Again, he was making a statement with the invitation, and so was I by insisting that I wouldn't meet with him alone. He never bothered me again.

I always received my free tickets for being a Commissioner, but I never would accept additional tickets from promoters or anyone else. I wouldn't take the extra freebies; I always paid face value because I knew there would be some price involved or some favor expected.

I recall right after I was named to the Commission I was at a big fight at The Mirage, and I was sitting right below the ring when they introduced everybody. When they called out Don King's name there was this huge booing and catcalling, and King just sat there smiling with this demented smile, saying to those around him, "They love me, they love me…." He did that for about a minute, just smiling and waving the whole time. The guy truly loves himself, and I guess he assumes the whole world does too. I have to admit that, in his own odd way, King is rather charming.

No Denying It: Boxing is Big

It was enlightening being introduced to this seedy side of life. It was like being in a shark pool, where you just kind of dodge a little as they come by and hope you don't get bitten. But you have to understand that, in the big picture, boxing is absolutely huge in the economy of Las Vegas. It greatly affects the annual earnings of the working class as well as the hotels. A big fight always means good tips for cabbies, card dealers, and cocktail waitresses. When we turn down a big fight because our Commission has integrity, as happened in the Mike Tyson-Lennox Lewis fight because of the misconduct at the press conference, a lot of good people in our city take a hit in their pocketbooks. And yet it was a proud moment for the Nevada Athletic Commission. They did the right thing by not sanctioning that fight because Tyson was acting too bizarre. There was no telling what he'd have done once the bell rang.

And of course the big fights draw the biggest gamblers and the highest rollers, who use the fight as an excuse to fly in from all over the world to see the spectacle. But what a challenge it is to regulate it all, because the whole boxing world is riddled with fraud and cheating and stealing.

Marc Ratner, who is the executive director of the Commission and has given his heart and soul to it for 20 years, is an honorable guy and very effective in the job. He loves sports in general. He is a football referee and has done some Big 10 games and is just really good at what he does. Plus, he's a nice person. Every time I see Marc he gets mad at me for getting off the Commission. I did so when I ran for Nevada's lieutenant governor in 1994 because I didn't feel it would be ethical to hold a place on the Commission while I was asking hotel owners for money to run my campaign. I think the last fight I went to was the great Ear Buffet, when Tyson turned into Hannibal Lecter and bit a chunk out of Evander Holyfield.

A Chance to Give Back

In looking back at why I accepted the responsibility of the Commission, it wasn't that I loved boxing so much or was enamored by celebrities; it was just that Nevada has treated me so well over the years and I wanted an opportunity to give back. And I'd be lying if I didn't say that it was fascinating at times. I recall one moment that was pretty interesting, and pretty scary too. There was a heavyweight named Tony Tubbs. He had been nailed previously for cocaine possession, and he once failed a drug test with us. About a year later he was coming back to fight, if I remember correctly, Buster Mathis Jr. It was at the Union Plaza. He had tested himself a couple days before and the test was dirty, and that information became available to us. And then the test he took on Thursday was clean, so something was fishy. Anyway, it was my job to go down to the Union Plaza at the weigh-in for the fight and call Tony over to a corner of the room and tell him that he could not fight.

He got this wild look in his eye and said, "You're taking away my livelihood. I'm going to kill you right here." And I thought for a minute he might strangle me before anybody could do anything about it. That was a tense moment. At that very second I was kind of thinking that I didn't want to be a boxing commissioner.

Those guys are so big, and punch so hard, that it's unreal. I watched Tyson work out in a gym a few times, and his punch was so awesome that one hit on a regular guy could easily kill him. And another time I remember him jumping rope at a blinding pace for 20 minutes without stopping. There are no athletes that get in quite the shape as a top boxer.

I look back on that time on the Commission as just another way that I could give back to my community. I'm an activist and I get things done, and I like to think I helped that Commission become more businesslike and more professional, and that's a good feeling.

I'd be remiss if I didn't tip my cap to my good friends Dave Belding and Ken Fleming for sharing their immense boxing knowledge and their historical perspective about the sport with me during my time on the Commission.

Chapter 8

My Grandma Mimi

I wish I knew where Bruce gets his inner drive. Maybe it's natural curiosity or just the need and desire to grow and expand, but I know I've been inspired by him since we first met. — Mary Hamilton

I've had so many people that were great influences in my life; my fear is that I won't mention all of them in this book. But the one individual who clearly had the greatest impact on me as a mentor, role model, support system, and all-around character was my grandmother Lois Henderson, whom the family called Grandma Mimi.

Birth Control

When I think of her so many images flood through my mind that I'll start with a long list of who she was and what she did. Bear with me because the list is as long and colorful as her life:

Grandma Mimi was intimate, fascinating, vibrant and dynamic. She was a gypsy, a flapper, a trendsetter among her peers, and an activist long before it was popular. She believed in contraceptives and birth control and actually sold birth control devices from her many homes

as she moved around, from Big Bear to Barstow, Palm Springs to Las Vegas.

She believed in UFOs. She believed in reincarnation and was certain that in a prior life she was a soldier in Asia. She was a physical therapist and a chiropractor and a healer. She understood reflexology and could often tell what was wrong with people by touching their feet. She practiced chiropractic until she was 85 years old, and that's no easy profession for a woman who stood 4 foot 11 inches and weighed 100 pounds after a big meal.

She worked hard for her money, but didn't believe in hoarding it. She was as good a spender as she was an earner. When Sherry and I were first married she bought us a refrigerator for $1500. She couldn't pay for it in full, so she did it by making monthly

53

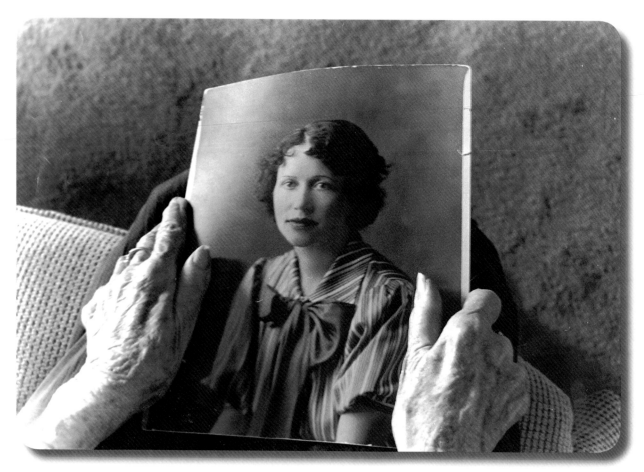

payments. She also bought me my first car, a blue 1963 Volkswagen with a convertible top. She also bought herself a new car every year, even though it was probably not the soundest thing for her to do financially.

Her wisdom was legendary among her friends. They were always coming to her for information or advice. She gave off the aura of someone who is all-knowing. She taught me to look for beauty in everything, whether it was the desert or sunrises or mountain peaks. She loved country music for its honesty and basic values. She particularly liked Eddie Arnold, and I have vivid memories of sitting out in the boondocks with her listening to "Make the World Go Away." She taught me to appreciate and love music. She was also a poet, and could recite verses from Edgar Allan Poe and Emily Dickinson. A lot of her recitations were of her own compositions, and she knew them all by heart. They were wonderful to listen to, because she was a mesmerizing speaker, whether it was poetry or history or sports or medicine. She would have been a five-time champion on *Jeopardy* and dazzled even Alex Trebeck had she been given the chance.

A Renaissance Woman

I honestly feel I learned three-quarters of what I know about life, philosophy, and spirituality from my grandmother. We have the same curiosity and passion for people. Interestingly, people have always come to me for advice and counseling, as they did with her, so there's some genetic pattern happening there.

Grandma Mimi always talked about how it was her destiny to help people, and she practiced that in her profession by taking a full schedule of about 12 patients a day and manipulating them on one of her chiropractic tables. It was unbelievable to watch, considering how small she was.

I remember when her husband Harley had broken his hip, and a physical therapist came to the house to help him. I noticed that the physical therapist was in pain as well, suffering from a bad back. When the therapist returned for a second appointment a few days later, I noticed that he was walking much better and I told him so.

He said, "Your grandmother just put me on the floor and gave me an adjustment, and I have never felt so good." The story isn't all that remarkable, until you realize that Grandma Mimi was 89 years old at the time.

But chiropractic was just part of what she did. She also sold real estate, had a health food store, and ran a 25-room motel, all at the same time.

There was one thing she didn't do well: cooking. She was just the worst cook; she always burned everything. I guess it was that she had so much on her mind and didn't have the patience to watch something on a stove.

Grandma Mimi was even somewhat responsible for my moving to Las Vegas. My mother didn't want to raise her kids in the smog of L.A., and Mimi had made frequent trips to Las Vegas to gamble and loved the place, so that's why we settled here.

Among the thousands of things she taught me, perhaps the most important were these: in order to understand the meaning of life I must remember to laugh deep and long, so hard that my eyes watered and I'd get stomach cramps, and to help people along the way. She said that laughter and a positive spirit will inspire others in a positive way, and the ripple effect of that warmth and exuberance will make the world a better place. She knew about paying it forward 50 years before the book was written.

Bruce has a way of putting people at ease with his smile, his comfort with himself, and it spills over to everyone around him. He is just happy in his own skin. — Sherry Layne

Grandma Mimi died eight years ago, but fortunately we have preserved her image and a sampling of her words on a video we made during a Thanksgiving dinner at our house in 1989. There she is at the dinner table, with a dozen family members around her, holding court. She had just been released from the hospital either that morning or the previous day, but she spoke as clearly and was as thought provoking at 90 as a person half her age. I showed the video to Jack Sheehan and he was blown away at her wisdom, her charisma, and how she commanded attention. As Jack pointed out, most people in their 10th decade become increasingly self-absorbed. They are concerned only with their own health, their mobility or lack thereof, their bowel movements, and how long they have left on the planet. But on that tape Mimi is sharing wisdom with all of us, talking about how positive thoughts and actions will have a ripple effect on all of those around us. It is as though she is a Kung Fu master, dispensing wisdom to all of her grasshoppers. I treasure having that tape, and wish we'd done even more of her, to capture and pass down to generations of our family her knowledge and common sense.

I still think about Mimi and miss her every day.

Chapter 9

My Biggest Contribution

Ten percent of life is what is given to you; ninety percent is how you handle it. — BL

I've said it before, but the biggest contribution I've made to the Las Vegas community is through the 50 some speeches I've given to high school and college students over the last 25 years.

When we first set up Career Day at UNLV, none of the deans would support us. They had that Ivory Tower mentality that the wisdom they were passing down was irrefutable, and they didn't want some outsiders perhaps coming in and giving contradictory information to their students.

I challenged them one day and said, "You guys are threatened, aren't you?" And I think that put them back on their heels a little. Eventually, they relented, and over 200 different classrooms opened their doors to outside speakers. UNLV's long-time director of development Fred Albrecht and I started that program and it was wonderful, but it was a real tough sell in the beginning.

Career Day for the seniors in the Clark County School District is another wonderful program. I have been in charge of that for six years. We give out scholarships and I am the keynote speaker. It's usually held each April, at the Palace Station, and I work with a dedicated woman named Joyce Woodhouse, who is the partnership coordinator for the Clark County School District. I start out by telling them that I'm going to talk about success and failure. I tell them about my failures and flaws and talk about how to be successful and I guarantee them that if they cultivate these six attributes, they will not only have a successful career but more importantly an enjoyable life.

I tell them to have a plan in writing. They have to create goals, and putting it in writing makes them accountable. Only about 20 percent have usually done this prior to my talk.

Then I talk about pursuing excellence and how they have to do their best. I recount how I got my CPCU accreditation with five years of studying and taking national exams. And I provide anecdotes, like the one about the guys laying bricks for a church. The first guy says, "I am

57

laying bricks for this building," and the second one says, "I am building a cathedral." That points out pride in workmanship.

Next I talk about the importance of a positive attitude and perseverance. I talk about how I flunked out of UNLV my first year, and the lesson I learned from that, and also what I learned from my failed bid for lieutenant governor. They enjoy hearing about the political experiences.

Then I go into the importance of having people skills and communication skills. Whatever business they are in, they will be dealing on a daily basis with people. I explain how they can utilize relationships and how much satisfaction can be derived from inspiring people.

Attitude is Everything

I talk about how they need to work on being a good listener and a good writer and a good speaker, but most importantly, a good listener. I talk about how in our office

I set up a speakers' bureau, where we would go out into the community and speak to groups.

We got this reputation of being responsive to issues and I was often called by the

newspapers, ever since 1984, to answer questions about insurance, sort of as a voice of authority. I explain that whatever you are doing in life involves communication skills and the art of persuading people, whether it's trying to get a job or trying to get a date.

And I discuss the importance of being well rounded. You have to have a balance in life. I wasn't impressed by someone who just studied all the time and had an "A" average. I was more interested in the person with a "B" average who was also socially adaptable, athletic, and cared about the community. The attitude was so important.

I also talk about the principles that are not taught or emphasized enough in school: honesty, work ethic, and fairness, and I usually define what those are. Then I close by giving them the four most important books that have influenced my life and helped me enjoy things that I have accomplished. Those are *Learned Optimism*, *The Art of Happiness*, *The Power of Now*, and *Ten Fun Things to Do Before You Die*.

I love to get interaction going in the classroom about the definition of success and what it really means. Some of the questions the kids ask are interesting.

"Is money that important?" Is one that usually comes up.

Or "How do you handle ethics?" That question is not surprising in these days of CEO greed and corruption at the highest level of public companies. With Enron and Martha Stewart and the like constantly in the evening news, young people rightly question the role of ethics in business. And my answer is that you just have to be in control and constantly avoid looking at matters in a self-centered way. Too many people in the business world are self-centered and focused on "What's in it for me?" I emphasize the importance of having a moral code and never wavering from it. In every instance, a businessman must ask himself, "Is this the right thing to do? Is this strategy or financial decision fair to everyone?"

I am also often asked, "How do you motivate and inspire people?" And the answer is, "By example. By not asking a person to do something you're not willing to do yourself."

I tell kids that life is ten percent of what you're born with and 90 percent what you do with it. I explain that every student in the room has the power to elevate himself to a higher level through hard work, advanced education, and adherence to a strong moral code.

I think kids today are more interested in a balanced life than one in which their career becomes everything. I asked my son Chad five years ago, and then again two years ago, whether he'd be interested in buying the agency or taking it over when I was ready to sell. I told him I'd sell to him for almost nothing. And he said, "Dad, I want more balance in life than you had."

And I understand that. It was not much fun waking up at two in the morning and worrying about whether I could make payroll, or whether we were going to lose a certain account.

Between the Clark County School districts and UNLV Career Days and subsequent visits to classes, I figure that I have lectured to over 4,000 kids in Clark County, and I think that I've had a positive effect on them. You have some kids, of course, who don't hear the message, but I think I had an impact on at least 10 percent of them, which would be 400 kids. If I reached half of them, then so much the better.

I sponsored six Career Day breakfasts for high school students; I also gave out $20,000 over six years in scholarship money to high school seniors for the best essays describing career goals and aspirations. I donated about $120,000 to UNLV over the years, which attests to my commitment to Paying It Forward.

Some of these participants in the early years of Career Day are now employers extending the same opportunity to today's seniors. — Clark County School District

Student Feedback

Here are a few samples of feedback we received from the students following my presentations:

I give much thanks to Mr. Bruce Layne for his deliverance of the three steps to success: goals, excellence, and helping others.
— *Emily Affleck, Las Vegas High School, 1998*

When the words of Eleanor Roosevelt were shared with me, that 'the future belongs to those who believe in the beauty of their dreams,' I realized that these are not simply the things that find a way into your head every single night, but those extra moments you hide somewhere and hope that one day they will come true.
— *Sasa Nikolic, Valley High School, 1999*

A wise man once said, 'The recipe for life is a spreadsheet of goals and aspirations, always finding the drive to pursue excellence, a positive attitude, a pinch of will power, a tablespoon of people and listening skills, assorted principals in order of importance, and topped off with a dash of disciplined work ethic. Bake these ingredients for years and age them to perfection and the end result is a delicious life served on a platter.' This wise man is Mr. Bruce Layne. He is an inspiration to many who, like himself, are equipped with an unbreakable spirit to survive this stressful world.
— *Jami Lampkins, Las Vegas Academy, 2002*

Ten percent of life is what is given to you; ninety percent is how you handle it." As I sat listening to Mr. Bruce Layne recite the words of Mark Twain early that Friday morning, I thought how true that statement really was. After being rejected from the university I had wanted to attend since the fifth grade, I was feeling like a failure. I thought that all the hard work I had done throughout four years of high school — honor roll, cheer leading captain, and yearbook editor

59

— meant nothing. I had to settle for a university that in my eyes was nothing too prestigious. I took what was given to me, but I was not pleased.

I decided right then and there that, instead of pouting about my rejection, I would embrace what was given to me and, as Mr. Layne put it, "pursue excellence." As I approached the University of Nevada School of Medicine to meet Dr. Isralian, I was suddenly overcome with excitement. I would get to spend the day doing what I have always wanted to do — help people. The

Flight for Life helicopter soared over my head, and I suddenly realized that this was real.
— Angela Mucci, Durango High School, 2002

Chapter 10
The Imperative of Friendship

If it's true that a man's worth is measured by his friends, then I am wealthy indeed.—BL

I have about 20 people I consider close friends, and a bunch more I would call good friends. And then there are eight friends that I've known for close to 50 years. These include Bob Miller, Tito Tiberti, R.J. Heher, Linda Falba, Mike Hastings, Timbuck Rivera, Louisa McDonald, and Sherman Simmons. Whenever I talk to one of my lifelong friends I still feel the warm vibes even if we haven't spoken in six months or a year. Okay, so I'm an admitted friend junkie. There, I've come out of the closet. That feels better.

Friendship is one of those wonderful aspects of life that can be taken for granted if we're not careful. But friends are truly priceless and should be cherished. They can help you through difficult times, and I know they've certainly helped me through some rough spots. In turn, I've made an effort to always be there for any of my friends who have needed *my* help. Friendships offer us warmth, enjoyment, energy, and laughter. When I think of my friends the movie *The Big Chill* comes to mind. The whole idea of spending weekends with friends and dancing and eating home cooked meals and

*Tito, Louise, Bruce and RJ (top center).
Tito, Dugall Morrison, Mike Hastings, R.J. Her, Bruce Layne, Bob Miller (right). R.J. Heher, Bruce, Tito, Linda, Louisa, Father McLay, Timbuck (left).*

sharing experiences and ideas is really appealing. I know for certain that writing this book and reading the comments my friends have offered has made me appreciate them even more.

I guess it comes down to the fact that I've enjoyed sharing with people throughout my life, back to when I shared toys as a kid. I was never the type of kid who wanted to take my train set and go into another room and play with it by myself. I enjoy interaction with other people. And that never changes. As we get older we share experiences with others, go on trips with friends, and get together regularly at social events and parties. Maybe desiring friendship and companionship as much as I do can be a curse, because the commitment of time can be overwhelming, but I've never looked at it that way.

A friendship has to be a mutual effort, but if I like someone I meet I'll make the effort to ignite a friendship. I think people see immediately that I'm safe, and that I mean no harm. People sense very quickly that they can call me and that I'll be accessible. Maybe it comes from an inherent curiosity about human nature. I love to meet people, and I always want to find out more about each one by asking a lot of questions. They sense, I think, that I truly find them important.

The Nature of Politics

When I was campaigning for lieutenant governor, I found it very comfortable to "work" a room full of strangers. I might engage someone for 30 seconds or a minute, and then move on the run without offending the person to whom I was speaking. I remember a fellow employee asked me

Ken Fleming and Bruce

BRUCE
LAYNE
For Lieutenant Governor

▼
"Our number one enemy is violent crime."

A

SUCCESSFUL

BUSINESSMAN

♦

STRONG

ON

NEVADA

BRUCE LAYNE
For Lieutenant Governor

Bruce Layne, 48, has served as a successful business and community leader for many years. While he is new to politics, he is not new to Nevada. A resident since 1956, he has the credentials for the important responsibilities of Lt. Governor. He is president of the successful insurance firm of Layne & Associates, employing more than 50 people. He was vice-chairman of the Nevada Athletic Commission, served as a lay member of the State Bar Disciplinary Committee, and was founding president of Southern Nevada Clean Communities.

Layne will bring these business skills to office to promote a strong Nevada. With no tolerance for crime, support for a well-trained work force, and wanting to put a halt to government waste, Layne is dedicated to the community. He knows the issues. He'll get the job done.

▶ *"Our number one asset is quality education."*

"State government should live by the rules of responsible spending... just like we all do at home."
▲

Bruce, Sherry, Barbara Bush, President Bush and Trevor

once to show him how to work a room and make business contacts, and he told me later that he would be embarrassed when I would introduce myself, ask a couple quick questions of someone, then walk away and talk to someone else. But that was just my way, whether it was a political rally in which I was trying to get votes or simply a meeting of UNLV boosters. I could do it somehow without being irritating. I felt I could project my true personality in a brief conversation.

While I'm thinking about the campaign, my friend and co-worker Bill Wright, who ran my campaign after some initial blunders, reminded me recently that I had raised $350,000 early on, mainly in small increments of $500 and $1,000. I also put $150,000 of my own money into the coffers, but unfortunately we spent most of that too early in the campaign, before voters were really focused on the election. Bill also reminded me that I made a total of 140 appearances looking for votes, and I gave 110 speeches. I certainly didn't lose from lack of effort. Regardless of the outcome and what some would perceive my naiveté in politics, I'm still glad I ran for office.

I learned a lot about loyalty and the nature of friendship through that experience.

Like him or not, Bill Clinton is considered by many to be the consummate politician and maybe the best in history at working a room. He is instantly non-threatening and approachable, and when he shakes a person's hand he often takes it in both of his hands; he makes eye contact with whomever he is speaking. Many call him the most charming President we've ever had, even those who didn't vote for him.

Why Friendship is so Wonderful

It doesn't cost a cent
It is available to all ages
It makes those involved feel connected to
    one another
It makes us feel good about ourselves
It gives us comfort in hard times
It can begin in an instant
It can last a lifetime
It can change your life forever

— *The Book of Friendship*

Sandy Miller, President Bill Clinton, and Governor Bob Miller

What Goes Around

I'm not self-absorbed. I'm a big believer in Karma — that what you pass around you'll get back. That's a really practical concept in business: the customer will be loyal to the business that uses fair practices and doesn't try to take advantage. It's also very important in relationships: giving freely of one's own time and effort is almost always rewarded in kind. I like to help older people and kids, people who can't help themselves. That's why I love to share with kids the things that school won't teach. I just get a deep and real satisfaction from giving kids inspiration and guidance. Maybe it's Grandma Mimi working through me. I always get energized when I talk to my buddies, and I'm continuously curious about people, so that's why I keep acquiring friends as I go along.

Friendship means a lot of things, but at its base it means you feel a connection with people. With a friend, there's a lot that's quickly understood without talking about it. You can read their mind most of the time. If you constantly wonder what makes a person tick, or find their behavior odd or quirky, you are probably not going to bond.

There was always a tricky balance when I made friends with clients. I never believed in buying people off with lunches or dinners or Christmas presents, as some competitors did. It just happened naturally, where I'd be amused by someone or respect the way they conducted themselves. Or maybe I was merely interested in the way they managed their lives.

With my men friends, we talk about sports, about women, about triumphs and failures in business, about our kids and grand kids, about our responsibilities as husbands and fathers. And I love to needle and get needled. It's sort of a locker room thing with guys; towel snapping and jabbing. Women are a different breed of cat, and a lot of men have a tough time making friends with a woman without the other stuff getting in the way. It's the old *When Harry Met Sally* dilemma. Is it possible for a man to be close friends with a woman without wanting to sleep with her? I believe it is. It still comes down to feeling a connection and having trust. It's nice to know that someone has your back.

There are probably 12 to 20 people I could really trust in a pinch, friends like Bill Wright and Leo Seevers and John Glenn and Craig Sullivan. I know the old line about being able to count your really close friends on two fingers, but with me I'd have to remove my socks and start counting toes. And I don't take that for granted. I feel tremendously blessed to have that wealth of friendships.

Maybe it's some neurotic need that I have. I'm not sure. I'm almost embarrassed when I think about it. Maybe I'm just a friend slut.

I'm proud that I could go to either one of my sons and talk about anything. They really get it. Not all kids do. Both Chad and Trevor have a healthy outlook on life, and I'm very pleased about that. My sons think sometimes that I'm a bucket mouth, meaning that I share too much information about myself with people. They'll say, "Dad, you shouldn't talk about that!" And I guess sometimes I say things that shouldn't be said. I probably wouldn't have made a very good CIA agent. They'll tell me, "No one was supposed to know!" But I went and told them anyway. Like I said, I like to share.

Perhaps one reason I've made so many friendships that I treasure is that I have good common sense, and people seek me out for my opinion. When you share something personal or troubling or deeply important with someone, the ties of friendship are pulled tighter. I've even had people ask me whether they should have a third child. And they followed my advice and had one! Again, that probably comes from my Grandmother Mimi, the fortune-teller and healer. Chad gives me a hard time about sticking my nose in other people's business, but it's not that I seek out personal stuff; it's that it seems to come to me. And I actually enjoy being approachable and listening to people's problems and concerns.

Friendships are how we connect with the world.
The people we enjoy at work and at play, on the social scene or in service to others, at home and away, enrich our lives and promote our well being, even our health.
And we do the same for them!

What a pleasure it is to have good friends,
even a best friend or two! With friends, we share tasks,
plan ahead, gossip, and laugh out loud.
Truly, it is a blessing to have friends, and to be one.
— Introduction to The Book of Friendship

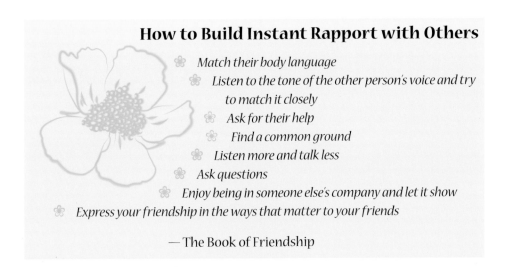

How to Build Instant Rapport with Others

❀ *Match their body language*
❀ *Listen to the tone of the other person's voice and try to match it closely*
❀ *Ask for their help*
❀ *Find a common ground*
❀ *Listen more and talk less*
❀ *Ask questions*
❀ *Enjoy being in someone else's company and let it show*
❀ *Express your friendship in the ways that matter to your friends*

— The Book of Friendship

Afterword

You are a good friend and a poor politician. Those are two very fine attributes. — Ken Fleming

Writing this book has been an amazing challenge, but one that is worthwhile on many different levels. Like many projects I've been involved in, it started with an idea that grew into something much more demanding than my original thought. I'd encourage anyone who ever uttered the words, "I ought to write a book," to give it a shot. The process turns into a wonderful self-revelation and self-discovery.

The process of putting all this down on paper has made me reflect on my whole life: the good, the bad, and the ugly, but mostly the good. It has caused me to dig deep to reflect on all the various stages of my life, including an upbringing in which our family broke apart. And getting my brothers' observations on that period of time has certainly been revealing, and hopefully healing. I was surprised at how many of my life-long friends placed an emphasis on the family split-up. I just accepted it at the time as something that happened and tried to press on.

My initial thought was that I wanted the book to be inspirational, for people to perhaps see that if I got over all these obstacles and hurdles and setbacks that life throws in our paths, then they can too. How often do we hear of people blaming early family problems for their failures as adults? It's my feeling that anyone who needs an excuse can always look hard and find one. I've always preferred to avoid excuses, and I made up my mind long ago to be unbeatable and not to give in to anything.

When you sit down and write out all the obstacles that you face in life, as I have done, I can look at the list now and I'm not sure they were obstacles at all. I certainly didn't treat them as though they were.

I believe self-absorption is best treated by helping others and performing selfless acts. I know that when I gave employees unexpected bonuses, or shared the wealth with them when the company did well, it gave me far more satisfaction than spending the money on myself.

It's a big achievement to dig all this out, but I'm hoping the book will function as one more directional signal for my grandchildren and future grandchildren as they go through their lives. Maybe it can serve as a checkpoint, if you will, so when they get lost as we all inevitably do, they can read this and see what their grandfather did in a similar situation.

It is rather ironic that I'm choosing to use this book as a way to pass wisdom and experience on to my grandchildren, when so much of the wisdom I received came from my grandmother. Maybe I'm providing some sort of connection between these neat people in my family who are separated by four generations.

I know in prioritizing where I go from here, I want to spend more time with my kids and grandkids and raise the "savoring factor" from a 7 to a 10. I want to teach them to care more about their own lives and the lives of their friends and associates. I believe that caring is an instinct, but it's also a learned behavior. I also want to study more about human nature and the drive to succeed. How do people get inner drive? And why don't more people have it?

67

One of my biggest goals at this point is to make progress in the Parkinson's disease field. Our local group is just getting going, and I want to do everything I can to raise money and awareness. In just the first weeks the small group we've assembled has built a web site and printed a brochure that will be available at all doctors' offices. We have to build a bank of addresses and phone numbers of people in the Las Vegas area fighting Parkinson's. The doctors here, and the national statistics, say that there are about 8,000 people in Southern Nevada who have the disease. And yet one of the two national organizations has identified only 300 people, and the other 500. Obviously, the vast majority of people living here with Parkinson's have no support group and don't even know their condition. There are all sorts of issues, including depression and suicide, that afflict Parkinson's sufferers, and a lot of that can be addressed once we establish a bank of names of people who need support. So the activism I've always felt inside of me now has a new outlet and a new direction.

Perhaps the biggest payback I've gotten out of this project is reading all the thoughts of my family and friends. In addition to being included in this book, all of them will be placed unedited into a huge scrapbook. These testimonials have truly become a book unto themselves. I know I drove Jack Sheehan crazy by adding additional names by the dozens once we were underway, but even Jack finally admitted that their stories took on a life of their own and added an important dimension to the book.

"The most amazing thing of all," he said, "was that you had 50 people who would take the time to say nice things about you. The average man on the street would be lucky if he could get three people to do it."

It goes without saying that all my friends knew deep down that if they didn't say nice things they would be edited out of the book, but nevertheless I feel extremely blessed to have such an abundance of great people around me. If it's true that a man's worth is measured by his friends, then I am wealthy indeed.

Introduction
To Reflections from Family and Friends

If you've read everything thus far, then you know I'm a friend junkie. So when Jack and I started drawing up a blueprint for my memoirs, I knew I wanted several of my friends to participate and share thoughts and anecdotes. Jack agreed that would be a good idea, and suggested we get about 10 or 12 friends to participate. But of course we needed to include my immediate family members, and my brothers and mom, and my wonderful daughter-in-law Diane, to whom I'm as close as any father is to his daughter.

Jack got nervous when the list of contributors crept over 20. He warned me that his original idea of using the comments within the chapters of the book as spacing devices was going to be impossible with the number and length of them as they started to come in. But he hadn't seen anything yet.

I realized I wanted several of the guys in my TEC leadership group to share their observations, and then there were a couple of friends who had Parkinson's, like Jim Williams and Dennis Finfrock, that I knew could make important contributions. And what about my fellow workers from the days of Layne & Associates, who are still with me since the sale to Brown and Brown? They would certainly have something significant to add. Well, at the end of the day we had around 50 different voices who took the time and effort to be part of my book. Jack was beside himself.

But seeing as he had interviewed most of the contributors himself, either over the phone or in person, he began to understand my point: that just as a jury can form a valid opinion by listening to the testimony of a number of witnesses, so can a person's life best be examined by hearing from all those who have been a part of it. And Jack admitted to me that he was extremely impressed by the quality of my friends and family, and how much he enjoyed talking to all of them.

And so the personal reflections really became a book unto themselves, and rather than using these stories as spacing devices, we instead chose various salient points from several of them and used them as epigraphs for the individual chapters. We decided that the original comments were valid enough to stand alone as the second part of the book. So here they are.

I must say that reading them was the most enjoyable and rewarding part of this endeavor. There were so many wonderful surprises. I felt like Tom Sawyer, enjoying his own eulogy from the back of the church.

— Steve DuCharme, that rascal, as usual captured me and stuck it to me at the same time. He treated the assignment so seriously that he actually composed four different drafts until he was satisfied that he had adequately harpooned me. I can't believe I'm actually letting that smart ass roast me again, "in front of my back."

— Curt Anderson was profound, succinct, and right to the point, just like a great tax man should be.

— Mike Hastings really surprised me with the revelation that I had been an inspiration to him when he was struggling with his athletic career in college. To be remembered like that by one of the best high school athletes ever to come out of Las Vegas was a real thrill.

— Pam Newell admitted to me some 12 years after we became friends that she had seen me speak to her class at UNLV and how my message had really hit home. That was a nice surprise.

— Linda Falba. What can I say about dear Linda? Well, if you read her testimonial it might be that her memory is *too* good.

— Roger Taber had heard me talk about things a person should do before turning 40, one of which was to accumulate a lot of "Up Yours" money. And he took what I said to heart.

— Chub Drakulich should know that his words about the importance of my going back to school marked a major turning point in my life. Just at a time when I feared that my life was going nowhere, this good man gave me the kick in the butt that I needed to get back on track. How can I ever repay him for that?

— Susan Simmons and Diane Layne wrote straight from the heart, and I'll never forget the generosity of their words.

— Chad and Trevor reminded me with their reflections that Sherry and I did a pretty good job in the most important task of our lives, raising our children the right way.

— Sherry, the person who knows me best, wrote a beautiful testimonial that was right on the money. Jack said he didn't have to do any editing on her story, it was that good.

— Tim Layne, the little six-year-old that I helped raise, both shocked and impressed me with the depth of emotion he reached in recalling his challenging upbringing. His essay was almost like a therapy session, but I think it was good for him to get it all out, and I appreciate the gratitude he felt towards me.

— R.J. Heher's recollection of his Grandma Mannix, and how I always took time to speak to her, was especially heartwarming. We can learn a lot from the Indian and Oriental cultures on the way they respect their elders. Remember, older people have more life experiences than any of us and so many valuable lessons that can be passed down. R.J.'s story made me miss my grandmother Mimi all over again.

I could go on and pick out the favorites parts of all 50 of these pieces, but I'm afraid Jack would kill me. Editors like to tighten things up, and my inclination with my friends is to just go on and on.

I hope you all enjoy these thoughtful gifts as much as I did. — BL

Bruce at 2 or 3 years old

Sherry Layne

Thirty-three, going on thirty-four years ago, more than two thirds of my life, I met Bruce.

My father had moved to Las Vegas to work for Howard Hughes. We were living in the Sands Hotel and I was working as the first girl lifeguard on the Las Vegas Strip. A longtime friend was taking me to a softball game to meet a friend of her fiancé's. On the way to the bleachers of the baseball field to meet my blind date, Mary Jane's fiancé, Ron, ran into Bruce. As an aside to their conversation, we were introduced, and I went on my blind date for the evening.

The next day Bruce came out to the Frontier Hotel and we had a great visit, set a time for a date, and were inseparable the rest of the summer. His comfortable nature, easy to be with, was like a magnet for me. I was quiet and over-composed. He taught me to lighten up and laugh more. He had just graduated from college, he had no money, he owned an older navy blue Volkswagen, and had just bought his one and only suit. He had just started working for a bank and was full of enthusiasm and a quiet, innate knowledge that he would be successful.

My father was an executive with Howard Hughes. In the late 1960s Las Vegas was extravagant, splashy, and the executives were treated like kings. I was able to comp anything I wanted at any Hughes Hotel (Sands, Desert Inn, Silver Slipper, Castaways, and Frontier). Bruce and I went to all the show rooms, ate at the gourmet restaurants, and frequently visited the hotel lounges.

I remember that, after about two months of dating and being together most every night, Bruce

came to me and said, "I am having such a good time with you. I enjoy being with you so much, but, I can't afford the tips anymore!"

I grew up as an Air Force brat, moving around the world every three years. Long-time friendships were rare. I remember Bruce's taking me to the

movies during that first summer. It was an overwhelming experience when we walked in to find a seat. It seemed everyone in that theatre knew everyone else. It was so impressive for me to see how so many people went out of their way to say hello to Bruce. He was not only a magnet for me, but for most people. There was a way he put people at ease with his smile. His comfort with his own self spilled over to everyone around him. I wondered where he garnered such a wonderful attribute, that wonderful self-esteem he had acquired.
It was never a form of conceit; he is just happy in his own skin.

We had a whirlwind romance. Call it Kismet, call it made for each other, or as they say in today's world, call it soul mates — whatever it is — we were!

After 33 years of marriage there are far too many stories to recall here. We have been fortunate to have two extraordinary sons, a beloved daughter-in-law, and grandchildren that have brought overwhelming joy to our lives. The constants in our 33/34 years have been allowing each other to be individuals and supporting those passions and interests that we both have reached out for over the years. We have always respected and nurtured each other's feelings.

Bruce and I have been able to mix our love with an ability to be best friends.

Chad Layne

There are so many things I could say about my dad, but I'll try to keep it to a few memories that really stand out:

I appreciate now how he made me work elsewhere before joining Layne & Associates so that I could prove myself and earn my own way. That conveyed that he had confidence in me.

Growing up in the house on Rochelle, I remember one day eating with Dad at a Jack

in the Box. He told me that day that there was a rough point in his life when he had no money and that he was once in a fast food restaurant and asked for a cup of hot water so that he could pour ketchup in it and make tomato soup. Hearing that story, I knew that I wanted never to be broke. I was inspired to do all I could to succeed.

Also, when we were living on Rochelle, we would play HORSE a lot on our basketball court. He would let me win most of the time, but occasionally when he decided he needed to win a game he would go to his old reliable, the left-handed hook shot, and he was deadly with it.

One time as he was backing the car out of the driveway my foot was hanging out the door and he actually ran over it. I was in the eighth grade. I remember how he felt very guilty about that for a couple of weeks, and that stuck with me, that he was a compassionate person. I think his compassion and his love for people are big contributors to his success in business.

I also recall that he was able to receive both good and bad news and never lose his cool. No

matter what the situation, he always tries to positively analyze the situation and keep a level head about it.

Dad has always been a very positive person, and has always given me encouragement when I needed it. After low points in my life, such as the breakup with a long-time girlfriend, or situations at school or work, he would always give me motivational material to read or just call and leave a message to say "hi" and tell me he was thinking about me. That made all the difference in the world to me.

He understood that happiness was something that didn't come easily to me, and he clearly communicated that happiness was something that everyone has to work at, even him. Of all my friends, family, and acquaintances, I have never seen anyone that genuinely is more interested in people than my dad.

Dad has always instilled in me a respect for authority. If I came home and told him I was mad at a teacher, he would listen to my side of things and then tell me to respect authority.

He's the one who triggered my proposal to my wife Diane. I was telling him after dating her for four or five months how terrific she was and how maybe she was "the one." He replied, "Well, what are you waiting for?" And he encouraged me to start looking for rings.

To this day it's always more enjoyable for me to be involved with him in a sales situation or meeting a successful challenge at work. It's just more rewarding if he is involved.

He always likes to tell people that he was on "the six-and-a-half year plan at UNLV without the doctorate." He is very proud of the fact that, although he initially flunked out of UNLV, he came back from that disappointment and returned to college and graduated. He has a "classy pride" about things, meaning that he is extremely proud of his

successes, but never throws them in the faces of others. In fact he has offered financial support to numerous friends and family over the years without obligation.

There have been so many special trips with Dad. Here are some particularly memorable ones, in no particular order:

— The 1977 World Series, chanting "Reggie, Reggie!" when Reggie Jackson made two errors in the same game.

— A fishing trip with the Keatings. I remember watching Tom Keating and my dad playing pool in one of the lodges and thinking to myself, at a very young age, that these were two genuinely good men.

— Trips to Phoenix Suns games on a jet with Bob Miller, Dave Belding, and my dad.

— World Series 2000. Diane, Trevor, Dad and I went. I was sick as a dog, but still had a great time.

— A Florida trip when I got horribly sunburned and Dad was scraping the mosquitoes off me as

my skin was peeling off. Although that wasn't one of my favorite adventures, I can look back and laugh at the predicament.

— Basketball trips to watch the Rebels in the PCAA tournament. Always a lot of fun.

— An Alaskan fishing trip. What I remember most was Uncle Leo and Dad's breaking the sound barrier with their snoring.

— A Dodger-Pirate game when we went into the locker room after the game. The two things I'll never forget were: 1) Kent Tekulve being mean to Trevor and making him cry; and 2) Willie Stargell's penis. I think it hung to the floor!

Trevor Layne

Another time my entire class was taking a trip to Reno, and I was waffling on attending because of my homesickness problem. So Dad — either from love, pity, or embarrassment, I'm not sure which — dropped everything he had going on and went with me on the trip. I had the best time, and after that homesickness ceased to be a problem for me.

I admire many things about my father. I have never heard him talk negatively about anyone. He treats everyone with respect. He is also selfless, always giving his time to the community whether it's speaking, coaching, or just giving advice to those who ask. He is so patient, understanding, loving, generous, and attentive, and he has an inherent sense of fairness that's difficult to explain unless you witness it on a daily basis.

"Work, earn, set goals, and enjoy life to the fullest." That's

Trevor and Bruce, Alaska, 2001 (top right). Bruce and Chad, Alaska, 2001 (left); Bruce and Chad, San Diego Padres game, 1992 (bottom right).

Dad has always put the family's needs first. I was homesick when I was a kid, and my parents had the unfortunate obligation of picking me up at my friend's house at three in the morning when I decided I had to go home. That must have been a lot of fun for them, to hear the phone ringing at three a.m. and find out that I wanted them to come pick me up.

been his message to me from day one, and he's never pushed or pressured me into doing something. He's only encouraged and supported what I wanted and taught me to be the best at that.

My dad has always been there for me and always will be, no matter what hand fate has for him. He's shown me that the more obstacles we face, the stronger we will become, and that we learn our most valuable lessons from our worst defeats and failures. He really loved sports when he was younger and excelled at baseball. The funny thing about that game is that you can fail 7 times out of 10 and still be considered one of the best in the game. A .300 batting average over a long career will probably get a player in the Hall of Fame. Sometimes our concept of success gets warped and we think we've failed, when actually we've triumphed. My dad's story is like that. He experienced heartache and failure early in his life, but eventually overcame everything life threw in his way.

Parkinson's disease is no different. He considers it just a small obstacle that needs to be overcome and conquered, and my dad's personality is such that he will walk away from it a better person and it will only make his life more fulfilling in the long run. Nothing can stop him once he decides he wants something. Nothing has been able to defeat him up to this point in his life, and seeing his drive and determination to contain and defeat this disease makes me believe this will be no different.

There are so many great memories through the years. Here are just a few:

— When I was little we would listen to 8-track tapes in the car on trips. I remember Roger Whitaker, Crystal Gayle, John Denver, Neil Diamond, and Crosby, Stills & Nash. I still like all of those.

Because we didn't have DVD players and video games in the car back then, we actually had to spend time in conversation and bonding with the family on these National Lampoon vacations. Our favorite song was Jim Morrison and the Doors "Break on Through." The lyrics embody my dad's philosophy that nothing stands in the way when you really want something. Once he sets his mind on something, as the saying goes, "It's all over, Johnny!"

— I remember playing catch with him all the time as we watched Monday Night Football. He was always very unselfish with his time, and made sure he took individual trips with me and Chad, so we could have that special one-on-one time together and really bond as only a father and son can.

— In the movie Glengarry Glenn Ross we saw that 90 percent of salespeople quit their first year. And even though Dad chose an extremely difficult profession — selling insurance — he had the drive, the personality, the discipline, the work ethic, and the passion to overcome rejection and succeed. He still has that today and that keeps my parents' marriage together after all these years. It is these characteristics that eventually will help him kick Parkinson's ass, just like everything else he's done.

— To use another movie analogy, I feel like I'm the Karate Kid and my dad is the Sensei, the Pat Morita character. He has the wisdom, and, as I soak it up, I become stronger and more noble and able to take on the world.

— The older I get, the more I appreciate how important the family is for survival and endurance in this dog-eat-dog world. And I respect and am so thankful for the relationship I have with my dad.

Diane Layne

(Chad's wife, Bruce's daughter-in-law, in a personal letter to Bruce)

When I first heard that you had Parkinson's, my hope was that it was a minor illness that would be very slow in progressing. And of course I worried about Chad and how he would take the news. He's so close to you and relies on you so much.

I felt that my relationship with you became even stronger with the news because this meant we had yet another thing in common, since my diagnosis with lupus. I knew that we now shared all the emotions and feelings that you go through when you first find out that you have a disease. There is so much that goes through your mind:

— A need for any and all information about the illness.

— A fear of not being there for your loved ones.

— A compulsion to took back on your life and realize everything that you have done and still want to do.

— An awareness that the sun is still shining and that you are determined to fight and live on, never giving up.

I think that you comforted us as much or even more than we consoled you early on. You perked right up after a couple days and took charge and started taking all the positive steps necessary to make the situation better. You spoke to many other people with Parkinson's. You read everything there was to read. You visited numerous doctors. And as you consumed all this information you shared it with your family, which helped us a great deal. You were ready and willing to try different things, from a minor sacrifice like not eating ice cream (I guess that isn't a small thing for you — ha, ha) to exercising more, to massages, to vitamins, herbs, medications, experimental approaches, etc. You were in the beginning and still are unstoppable. I believe that you have definitely slowed the

Chad, Barbara Bush, Diane, and Bruce

progression of the disease by all your efforts, and that you will be one of the first to take part in finding a cure for Parkinson's.

I feel that, of all the people I know, if I could pick just one person that the world needed as a mentor, or if I were to choose an ambassador for spreading wisdom and joy and humor, that person would be Bruce Layne. I just know in my heart that, with your indomitable spirit, you will conquer this disease and we will be blessed with your presence for a long, long time. You will be there for us years from now to offer encouraging words, a positive outlook, a shoulder to lean on, and always ... always a good laugh.

I love you! Diane

Tim Layne
(Bruce's little brother)

At the age of four I was allowed to return to Las Vegas to live with Doc (my father) and Bruce. My mother had remarried and things were not working out too well for me with them.

The following years, from age four to eight, I lived with Doc, Bruce and Jim (for a little while until he was drafted into the service). Bruce became my unofficial guardian upon his return from CSUF. He took me to all his baseball practices and his games. Bruce played first base for the Running Rebels.

During these years Bruce had lots of different jobs; he was 19 at the time. His shortest-lived job was working for Delta Maintenance cleaning public rest rooms. He lasted three days. I think it was a nightmare for him. He also had a job working at an ice-cream store; unfortunately for me, that job lasted only about a month.

Another of Bruce's more steady jobs was working at a titanium plant. This was an evening job that provided him with free, unbreakable, prescription safety glasses. He used these glasses for

baseball, and they lasted until he was hit in the head during a game by a bad pitch.

My favorite of Bruce's jobs while I lived with him was working as a pool boy at the Riviera Hotel. I lived with my Dad (Doc) and Bruce from kindergarten through the first half of third grade. This was great for me because the Riviera had what, at the time, was Las Vegas' best pool, and I could swim all day during the summer while he got paid setting people up around the pool with their towels and chaise lounges. Sometimes at the end of the day, when it wasn't crowded, he would come into the pool and launch me by my feet high in the air so I could do flips. I also helped out picking up towels and chaise lounges when the pool closed for the day.

One of my favorite drinks was (and still is) Hawaiian Punch. The only problem was that whenever I asked for, or said, "Hawaiian Punch," I would get punched. This game worked both ways, so I could always punch the other person if they said it too. Remember, I was much smaller than my brothers at this time, and their punches could be pretty painful. One summer when Jeff was visiting from San Francisco, Jeff, being six years older than me, had made me cry in a game of Hawaiian Punch that got out of control. Bruce, being more than six years older than Jeff, came into the room and evened the score by hitting Jeff hard enough to make him cry. You can imagine how I admired Bruce for looking out for me; I believed I was the luckiest boy on earth having Bruce for my brother.

Another time, when we were driving somewhere with Bernadette (Bruce's girlfriend) and possibly her sisters and my other brother Jeff, a car with some jerks pulled up alongside at a stoplight. These guys said something threatening to Bruce and one of them held up a tire iron or pipe. Bruce, without hesitation, stepped out of the car, ripped the weapon out of his hands, hit the guy, hopped back in the car and we drove off.

Bruce used to take me everywhere with him, and I loved tagging along. Bruce never made me feel unwanted; I felt that he enjoyed my company. That says a lot, considering Bruce was just barely an adult himself and he had to take care of me, too.

— One year I returned home after a summer vacation with my mother and stepfather in San Francisco to find that Bruce and Doc had moved. I missed the old house and begged Bruce to take me over there. Seems that the house had been vandalized: some of the interior walls were knocked down with baseball bats that Bruce and his friends had used. I think this was in response to being forced out of the house due to foreclosure.

The new house was a rental and there was a fig tree near the back door. In the fall it dumped a lot of rotten figs on the ground and then leaves fell on top of the figs. This became an ideal breeding ground for the Las Vegas cockroaches. When we would come home at night you could see and hear them scurrying across the sidewalk and under the leaves as we approached the back door. We would take a shovel or broom and pound the ground to kill them and then run in fear that they might organize some sort of counterattack.

Bruce always seemed to be the one to catch me when I was getting into trouble. Like the time he caught me playing with matches outside the window of our bedroom. We had a small metal trash receptacle, the type where the lid opens when you press on the foot pedal at the bottom. I was learning basic principles of combustion (by myself of course) by placing burning objects inside the trash receptacle and then lowering the lid to smother out the fire. It wasn't until I decided to see how a plastic garment bag from the dry cleaners would burn that the smell was so overwhelming that Bruce investigated by looking out the window. When Bruce questioned me about lighting fires, something I obviously knew I wasn't supposed to be doing, I responded like most seven year olds and said, "No, I am not lighting fires." Although I was quick to drop the lid on the garbage can, I didn't look too innocent standing there with a book of matches in my hand.

Bruce got the scar on his shoulder playing with Jeff and me. I had received a bag of marbles as a gift, and Jeff and I were tossing the bag around. Somehow the bag of marbles went through the window, which broke into many shards. Soon thereafter I was creeping around the outside of the house, trying to remain undetected (it was part of a game) when Bruce saw me while looking through the broken window. He raised his hand up to hit me with a water balloon and in the process, impaled his shoulder on a piece of glass that was still hanging from the window frame.

Bruce, Jeff, and Jimmy at Disneyland

Another time, when I was nine, a friend and I were throwing dirt clods from my back yard against the wall of a business across the street to see them explode from the impact. When the proprietor of the business looked to see what we were doing to his back wall, he ordered my friend and me to stand in the back room of his shop while he called the police. Fortunately, Bruce came driving home before the police arrived. I saw him and called out to him. He came over, and I explained to him why I was being held inside this guy's back room. Bruce told us to get out of there, and while he was reading this jerk the riot act for abducting us, we ran over to my friend's house.

My Departure from Las Vegas, Doc and Bruce

Bernadette's mother had decided that she needed to know just what was going on between Bruce and Bernadette when they were over at our house. She found me and sat me down and began what I can only describe now as an interrogation. I had never seen Bruce and Bernadette doing anything other than making out, and it is from watching their relationship that I learned how a man behaves toward a woman and how women react. I don't remember them ever being purposely unkind or cruel to each other; they seemed to be aware that each other's feelings should be respected. Anyway, after Bernadette's mother finished questioning me I was very shortly thereafter dispatched to my grandparents' home in Barstow. Bruce and Bob Miller, using Mrs. Miller's late model Riviera, drove me to Barstow, unbeknownst to Doc. I was instructed, "led to believe," that, if I didn't lie down on the floor in the back of the car, we might get caught and I would not be allowed to go on a vacation to my grandparents' house. The reality was that I was being taken away from Doc, Bruce and my life in Las Vegas to live with my grandparents. When I was finally told the truth about my change in living conditions, I was heartbroken. I longed for

my bachelor lifestyle and, most of all, I missed Bruce and Doc. I think I missed Bruce the most because he let me be involved in his life, and I was afraid I wouldn't get to have that again. As it turned out, that is exactly what did happen. My life with Bruce and Doc, as I knew it, had ended.

Jeff Layne

I'm not surprised that Bruce has been successful in the insurance business because he always had a clear plan about what he wanted to do. He's always been confident, demanding of himself, well organized, and loaded with charisma. He was never one to waste time or just sit around with his feet up. He was pretty driven growing up; whether it was playing baseball, or traveling with friends, or helping out with the family, there was always a great sense of purpose there.

I always have respected Bruce's devotion to our family. I'm six years younger, but I always remember him taking me everywhere and allowing me to tag along. One story that tells a little about him occurred when he would have been about 16 and I was 10. We were riding around in his car, and I think his girlfriend was in the front seat with him and she had some kid sisters in the car with me. There were six of us piled into the car. He turned onto a busy street, and I don't know whether he cut somebody off, but anyway, a car with two teenage boys honked at us and they flipped Bruce off.

Bruce was furious that they would do that with a bunch of kids in the car, so he raced after them and, when they stopped at a red light, jumped out and went up to their car and started yelling at them. And then he popped the guy in the passenger's seat a couple times. I mean he really smacked him. As I recall the guy had a bloody nose. And I remember thinking that wasn't the smartest thing he'd ever done because there were two of them and one of him and a bunch of us kids.

When he got back in the car, I said, "That wasn't really too smart, was it?" He didn't respond right away, and then he said to me, "If you really wanted to help you would have handed me a baseball bat out of the back seat."

I think the reason he did it was that he was outraged that these guys would do something that crude in front of kids, and it was also a chance for him to be sort of heroic in front of his girlfriend. Bruce has always liked the spotlight.

I remember another time when he was fed up with our older brother Jimmy, who is two years older than Bruce. Jimmy had done something out of line, and some resentment had been building up between the two of them. One night it exploded in the kitchen and they went at it. And all of us were chanting for Bruce to kick his butt. It's funny how certain memories stay with me, but I sure remember that night.

The one area where Bruce has disappointed me is the way he is handling his Parkinson's disease. It's a nerve disorder, and as a chiropractor I deal every day with people with nerve disorders. But he does not acknowledge that chiropractic can help him, and I believe it's his best hope. It's odd that our grandmother was a chiropractor and so was our dad and so am I, and yet Bruce totally disregards it as a science that can help him. He has a narrow view of our profession, and I guess he thinks it's just for back pain.

Oh, and there was the time he hit a home run to win his last college baseball game. I guess the guy was just born to be a hero.

Irene Mendelson
(Bruce's mom)

Bruce was always outstanding. From the second grade on at St. Anne's Grade School, he was one of the leaders in his class. And he had a great group of friends along the way,

with Bob Miller and Tito Tiberti. He was always well liked, not just by his classmates but by their parents as well.

I feel so fortunate that all my sons were loving, good people, considerate of others and each other. None of them ever got into any trouble. Bruce was especially considerate to his brothers, always taking them to ball games and, of course, caring for Tim for a year or two when he was unhappy living in San Francisco.

Bruce was a good athlete and an outstanding baseball player, and so was his older brother Jimmy. They played on the same team together, and in American Legion ball, and later on the American Legion people helped us when we were working to get Jim his full disability payments from the government.

I think part of the reason that Bruce was so successful with his insurance business was because he'd been in Las Vegas so long and had such a good reputation as an honest, committed person. There

was a tremendous trust built up in the community from all his friendships and good relationships with people.

All my sons are caring, considerate people, but Bruce is exceptional when it comes to being sensitive to people's feelings. He just has tremendous empathy for people's situations. I know how close he was to my mother, his Grandmother Mimi. We still talk about her all the time when the family gets together.

Bill Borellis
(Bruce's brother-in-law)

I am proud to be Bruce Layne's brother, and I do consider myself to be exactly that — a brother more than a brother-in-law. Certainly, through the years we've had our differences, as all family members do. Egos run wild sometimes, and we're both very competitive, yet our lives focus around a common set of principles and values. He's a genuinely good guy, and although I don't like him all of the time, I love him.

Bruce Layne has a lot of extremely positive traits — planning and goal-setting are two of them. Most of us set goals once a year, at New Year's or at the beginning of our business fiscal year, then maybe push them aside. Not Bruce. He's really driven, or motivated, by action plans and accomplishments. In fact Winston Churchill is one of his heroes for his intelligence and also for acting on his convictions. Please don't get me wrong; Bruce also knows how to have fun and appreciate the finer things in life.

Occasionally I have flashbacks of our early years together. In our 20s, we (Bruce, Bob Miller, Greg and Steve DuCharme, Mike Hastings, Tito Tiberti, Rossi Ralenkotter, myself, and a few others) let off steam by playing hoops a few evenings a week, then drinking some beer and being somewhat juvenile. Las Vegas was a reasonably small town in the late 60s, and many of the people in our little circle turned out to be both politically and financially instrumental in the city's growth.

Another event in our past together is particularly notable. It must have been in 1968 or 1969 — Bruce and Sher were just married. I had an accident in my car and was in dire need of transportation, so I asked them if I could borrow their car, a Volkswagon Bug. They loaned it to me and later that night I had an accident: a dog crossed my path on a two-lane road leading to Paradise Valley Country Club; I swerved to miss the dog and wrecked their car, their only car. Oops! They never asked for any repayment and were really only concerned with my health.

For the last 35-plus years Bruce and I have knocked on a lot of doors together, opened many, and closed some. He and Sher have been a part of the few who have always been there for me when I needed help. Very cool!

At times we've also been very much in each other's face. We're a couple of old jocks whose heads are still into sports, but our bodies don't cooperate the way they used to. I branched out into golf and Bruce chose tennis. Up until a few years ago we competed against each other in both sports annually, usually during the holiday season. Here's where Bruce's devilish side shows its face. He's really a rat sometimes, and when he has the advantage his dark side comes out. He consistently runs my tail ragged in tennis. I feel like the Tasmanian Devil — one moment reaching for his drop volleys, then in the next breath scrambling back to get his lob. Here I am completely exhausted, looking over at him standing there fresh as a daisy, smiling like a Cheshire cat, totally enjoying playing with me. For some reason I just couldn't get the same satisfaction out of our golf matches … how come?

So you see, the life of Robert Bruce Layne, the person, is active, always growing — there seems to be no room for being stagnant, for moving any way but forward. Isn't that what we all would like our lives to be like?

Fred Albrecht

I first got to know Bruce in the mid-1970s when he was on our UNLV Alumni Board and we worked together to start the Career Day Program. It was a program that allowed alums who were business leaders in the community to come into the classrooms at UNLV and speak to the students about career opportunities and options they might consider when they graduated.

We initially met with a lot of resistance from the deans. I remember one of them said, "Why would we want to let alums into our classrooms where they might tell our students something contrary to what we are teaching?"

Bruce was incredulous. He couldn't believe there would be resistance to this. And he simply said, "Because we represent the real world."

We started out with only about 12 professors allowing us into their classrooms, but the program quickly became so popular that after eight or nine years we were going into 150 classes. That original program grew into the Career Day Luncheon, where we would invite keynote speakers to address the students and the professors who'd cooperate with us. And then nearly all the professors wanted to be invited and ended up participating. I know that program has had a tremendous positive impact on a lot of students' lives.

Bruce also was instrumental in bringing in the Hilton Hotel Corporation and some local engineering companies to come in and speak to students about employment. He was just extremely active and a real visionary in bringing new programs and ideas to our attention, and he always wanted what was best for the students. I think his UNLV education is something he's always been extremely proud of, and it was his way of paying back.

There's also a real fun side to Bruce. We used to go to the Flying Dutchman restaurant on Flamingo after some of our meetings, and there was a lot of laughing and joking. I remember a time when he had just bought a new Datsun 240 Z for Sherry. We'd had a few beverages, and when he was leaving he peeled out through the sand parking lot and bounced the car through a ditch. We kidded him that by the time Sherry got it, the 240 Z would be a used car.

There's another thing that bonds Bruce and me together. I was diagnosed with cancer of the head, neck, throat, and shoulders a little over two years ago, and was basically told there was no hope. But I didn't accept that verdict, and after defying death on more than one occasion I just decided I was going to beat this thing. My doctor told me 99.7 percent of all people would be dead with what I've gone through. I survived one blood clot that knocked me out for 15 minutes, and it was an actual miracle that I survived that. Through it all, I've never thought for a minute that I wouldn't survive.

So Bruce and I have both peeked over the edge in the last couple years, and we're both determined to not only survive, but to keep on living full lives and appreciating all our blessings and giving back to the causes that are important to us.

Ours is one of those friendships that has many layers and just gets richer through the years.

(Editor's Note: Ever the trooper, just as this book was going to press, Fred Albrecht accepted the interim Athletic Director's position at UNLV when John Robinson stepped down.)

Curt Anderson

Bruce Layne's discovery of Parkinson's disease is sort of the Horatio Alger story gone amuck. Here's this guy who works hard for years, builds a great business that is worth millions, has a great family, is able to sell the business for all the money he'll ever need, and then he has to wrestle this serious health problem. It's one of those reminders that life isn't fair. And yet through all of this Bruce has stayed very positive, is still involved in charitable causes, and very loyal to his original employees, many of whom benefited greatly with the sale of his company.

From everything I've seen, Bruce Layne is the real deal, and there aren't a whole lot of people you can say that about.

Dave Belding

Bruce and I go back to high school days when we competed against each other in sports. I was at Boulder City High, and he was a year ahead of me at Gorman. As I recall, we beat them in everything, but I think Bruce has a slightly different recollection.

When he was first contemplating a political run, he came to me looking for campaign money. I asked him what he was running for, and he told me Lieutenant Governor. So I asked him what the responsibilities of the job were, and he wasn't too sure. He said it had something to do with increasing tourism.

Then I asked him what political power the job held, and he didn't think it held much.

Next I asked him whether it was going to be a stepping stone to a higher position, and he said he hadn't given any thought to that.

So then I asked him about the pay, and he said there was no meaningful remuneration.

So I said, "Okay, it's essentially a position without power, that you are not using as a springboard to another position, and the job doesn't pay well. Why are you running, Bruce?"

And he said, "Well, Dave, this community and this state have been awfully good to me and I'd just like to give something back."

How could I turn down someone whose heart was in the right place and whose intentions were that pure?

So I gave him some money for his campaign, and it was straight downhill from that point forward.

Mike Benjamin

Bruce and I first met when he was running for Lieutenant Governor in the early 90s. I was impressed by his ethics, especially considering that he was a "politician." The two don't usually go together. Bruce is one of those people you go to when you need advice. It doesn't matter what kind, personal or professional; the insight and wisdom you can tap into are incredible. And he has the ability to relay it to you in such an insightful manner that what had previously seemed to be a tangle of loose ends suddenly comes together in a neat little package. He has a way of making big problems somehow seem much smaller.

When I first found out that Bruce had Parkinson's, he didn't tell me. Rather it came through the rumor mill at about 90 miles per hour. My first thought was to feel sorry for him, but I quickly realized he wasn't looking for sympathy, but rather saw the disease as a blessing. His inner drive to succeed, to excel at whatever life throws his way, resurfaced very quickly. I do feel that Parkinson's has changed his drive dramatically, but only the course his life takes, not the intensity of it.

Kella Brown

In the fable The Goose Story *an unknown author points out what science has discovered about why geese fly in a "V" formation. With each flap of its wings, a goose creates updraft for the bird immediately following it. It is estimated that by flying in a V formation, the whole flock has a 71% greater flying range than each bird would have flying solo. When the lead goose gets tired, he rotates backwards into the formation while another goose leads. The others honk encouragement from behind. When a goose gets sick or falls out, two geese drop out of the formation and follow him to the ground where they remain to help and protect their fallen confederate.*

I pick Bruce Layne to fly in my "V" formation.

Bruce is a smart businessman. His easy humor is grounded in intelligence. He is innately kind. He is hard working and persevering. He is good to his friends and remembers favors. He is disarmingly direct.

But, arguably, the most conspicuous thing about Bruce is that he is happy. Really. Not fake happy or trumped-up happy. Not moronically happy, and not happy in spite of his disease. Bruce is a happy guy who got Parkinson's, not a man who is able to feign happiness in the face of adversity. Bruce is authentically at peace from the inside out.

What an extraordinary quality for a leader! Stunning, really. Because he needs nothing from you to be at peace; he's positioned for clear thought and decisive action in the most tenuous of situations. The world just can't have nearly enough clear thought coupled with decisive action.

Bruce, I'm so happy to have you as a wing man. We all are. I hope the sweet fragrance of your friendship will be mine to enjoy for a long time.

Netty Capurro

Bruce has dealt with tremendous adversity in his life (Parkinson's being the most recent instance) and has come through a better person for it all. His gift is that he is, first off, an amazing survivor; and secondly, that his love and understanding of his fellow man has led him to try and help others survive, as well, through mentoring, teaching, and by his example. He is never condescending. He is never too tired to help, and yet he does not preach, nor does he offer pity. He is a teacher who has survived some real hard stuff and is eager to pass on the lessons he's learned. Deepak Chopra's got nothing on Bruce.

Randy Capurro

Unlike many others who knew Bruce, I was not shocked by his diagnosis of Parkinson's disease. For about six months prior to the news, people had been asking me about Bruce: "Is he all right?" or "What's wrong with Bruce? He was playing golf and he looked awkward."

So he came to me one morning with the news. I feigned shock and disbelief, mainly as a way of expressing sympathy, but I also knew he had already done a ton of research about the illness. He proceeded to tell me all kinds of possible scenarios. That is just his way. He always submerges himself in information, details, and other minutia.

Bruce told me where to go to find info about Parkinson's, which I did. We are always open and candid with each other, and he is every bit as important to me now as before his diagnosis, just different. I had already figured out that we must sell the company while we were on top. We needed to make this happen and we both began a process, led by Bill Wright, to merge or sell to the right people. Bill led the charge like a trooper. So did Dennis Stein. And we accomplished the impossible. All

Bruce's hard work, friendship, and honesty, all of his sacrifices and hardships were rewarded in the most positive manner.

Don Doyle

I've known Bruce for 17 years, having first met him through business. Our relationship quickly grew into a close personal friendship. Two years ago I was losing my mom; she was going into hospice to die, and I needed some guidance. Bruce was a great friend to lend an ear during that time and help me understand what was taking place and how to let go. He told me I had to talk to my mom constantly when I was with her, even though she was slipping in and out of a coma, and that's the exact same thing a hospice nurse told me.

The nurse said, "She can hear you; I don't know how, but she can." And sure enough, just two days before she died, she opened her eyes for a moment and said to my dad, whose name is also Don, "I love you, Don." And that was the last thing she ever said. Bruce was just a great friend during that time. When he and I have some central issues to discuss, we can cut right to it quickly. Those types of friends are rare.

Another time, two years ago, it looked like I was going to accept an opportunity to run a brokerage firm in Sacramento, where I would run some independent insurance agencies. It meant a move from San Francisco and I was excited about the opportunity, but then it didn't work out, and I was really disappointed. I called Bruce and was talking about it with him, and he said, "Why don't you come to Las Vegas and we'll discuss it face to face?" So I did, and we spent a great day together. We went out to his ranch and watched a foal come into the world, and it just helped me put things in perspective and realize that the river of my life was moving forward.

In the same way, he can confide in me about his challenges with Parkinson's. Friends like that, who can share the most personal issues, are wonderful to have.

Chub Drakulich

I first saw Bruce when he was playing baseball at Bishop Gorman High School. I was there scouting for Nevada Southern University. I liked what I saw. He was good, very good, and I definitely wanted to be his coach in college.

When Bruce had trouble his first semester in college and dropped out to work at the titanium plant, I went to see him. I really wanted him to play ball for us. I was able to offer him a Board of Regents Scholarship so he could afford to go to college. He rewarded my effort by hitting .395 that semester.

Playing ball at NSU was not as comfortable as playing ball at UNLV nowadays. We didn't have a baseball field. That meant we had to travel all over the city to practice wherever we could find an open field. It made practicing very difficult, but Bruce was always there, no matter what. Sometimes, when we would finally get to the other side of town to practice, we would get blown out or rained out and would have to turn around and just go back home.

It was such a pleasure being on the same field with Bruce. His sense of humor made for some very enjoyable and memorable practice sessions, as well as games.

I have two wonderful daughters, but I would love to have had a son like Bruce. I could always see that he was special. He was courteous, very industrious, and had respect for others. I retired in 1988 and haven't had much contact with Bruce until recently, when I was shocked to find out about his having Parkinson's disease. You just don't imagine that someone like Bruce would ever get something like that.

I think the one thing that makes me appreciate life the most is people. After that, it's being a mentor in the education field. Teachers get their satisfaction from their students' success. Being a recent recipient of a pacemaker also makes me appreciate the fact that I have another chance and more time to do the things I enjoy in life. I think Bruce appreciates people much the same as I do.

One of my favorite sayings is: "Excuses satisfy only the people who make them." Bruce isn't one to make excuses; he just jumps in and gets it done.

Steve DuCharme

I met Bruce in the fall of 1966 when I pledged what is now the Sigma Chi fraternity. It was difficult to pinpoint exactly when I first met him, because after you meet Bruce you feel as if you have known him forever. In the 60s there were no prohibitions against fraternity hazing by the actives (current members) against the pledges (prospective members). Chi Sigma Chi, as it was then known, was the "jock" fraternity on campus, as a number of the actives were either on the basketball or baseball team. Whether they were jocks or not, the actives were all Neanderthals when it came to harassing the pledges, and while Bruce did his bit to weed out the faint-hearted pledge, he did it with a smile and he was not mean-spirited.

At the end of the school year, in May of 1967, I became a summer replacement for one of Bruce's roommates, and we continued to share various apartments until his graduation in December of 1969. Bruce was a treat to watch operate. He held (and probably still does hold) the unofficial NCAA intercollegiate world's record for mooching consecutive meals without hitting the same place twice. Not only was he able to get his girlfriend du jour to paint his room and feed him, one sympathetic paramour bought him 10 or 12 sets of new underwear after watching him sift through a pile on the floor for his cleanest pair of holey shorts.

Bruce in the college years was very deceptive in his appearance. He looked like a big teddy bear, and while his speed in the 100-yard dash was clocked in minutes and his vertical leap measured in millimeters, he was an all-sport athlete. He had a scholarship to play baseball and he started on the fraternity's football and basketball teams. Bruce's basketball play defies explanation. He had one shot, and he called it his sky hook. While there was some hook to it, there was definitely no sky involved. As I mentioned earlier, Bruce was ground bound, so when he released the ball it was two and a half or three feet below the rim and had a trajectory as flat as Kansas. How the ball went in the basket is a physics enigma on par with Fermat's Theorem.

Bruce's ability to impress the opposite sex equally defied explanation: his success ratio was more than the sum of its parts (i.e. he didn't look like a movie star, he didn't have any money, his car was an old beater of a V.W. bug, and prior to Mary Jo his underwear had holes), yet he always had dates with the cheerleader, the homecoming queen, or the girl everybody else was dying to just talk to. I now attribute his romantic success to his non-threatening demeanor. Bruce has a kind heart, and it shows (this may be why he was so successful in the "n-charence bidness").

While the daughters loved Bruce, more often than not the mothers liked him more. That is why they were always feeding him and buying him clothes, and I suspect more than a few fathers slipped him a few bucks to cover expenses. They didn't think Bruce would take advantage of them, their daughter, or the situation. While the rest of us were testosterone-rising, go for the jugular, Playboy/Playmate obsessed horn-dogs, Bruce was a Jonathan Livingston Seagull-quoting wolf in-caring-compassionate helpmate's clothing. No one in our group ever heard of Rod McKuen until Bruce started getting dates by quoting him. Bruce was ahead of the curve when it came to getting in touch with his feminine side; in fact he was so far ahead of the curve he was around the bend. I say this because at some point we all noticed that Bruce would sit down on the toilet to take a leak. When asked about this he had various explanations, which included "I'm drunk, I'm fat, I'm lazy," all of which were highly plausible at the time.

Even with all that going on, none of us thought Bruce was "light in his loafers" (not that there is anything wrong with that), but some of us did begin to wonder if he was light in his Y chromosome when he began taking ballet lessons. The ballet lessons had us scratching our heads (mostly our heads) and Bruce said, "It's good for my timing, because I'm trying to perfect a crack-back block off the line of scrimmage" or some other such nonsense as that. Now all of his buddies started to imagine the then 200-plus pound Bruce in a room full of 90-pound "spinners," tossing them hither, dither, and yon. I can tell you that image was quickly chased out of our minds by a mental picture of Bruce wearing both a codpiece and a tutu, with his notorious calves (which are both the size and shape of the state of Illinois) encased in Danskin leotards (that thought was enough to put most of us off our feed for several weeks). But I'm not one to argue with success, and this feminine side stuff was definitely working for Bruce.

One of the more painful evenings of my life was spent on a ride out to Boulder Dam with Bruce. Bruce's summer job was as a lifeguard/poolboy at the Riviera Hotel (thanks to Bob Miller's dad Ross), and that enabled him to date tourists as well as the local talent. One day he came home and told me he had a date with a hotel guest who was a French tourist, and we should all take a ride to the dam. Let me tell you, there is not enough Coors beer this side of Golden, Colorado to compensate for 50 miles of Bruce talking baby talk in a French accent, while you are riding in the back of a non-air-conditioned VW with a leaky muffler.

Bruce's reign as a sandbagging Don Juan came to an end the night Sherry showed up at a fraternity party with Johnny Moran. Johnny was the anti-Bruce (i.e. he did look like a movie star, he had a new car, and he bought gasoline in increments larger than one dollar). Even with all that going for him, the next thing we heard from Johnny was, "What just happened here?" But Bruce never looked back. After having maligned Bruce's sincerity, it would still be my guess that all of those girls, and most definitely all of the mothers, have fond memories of their relationship with Bruce. But it was clear to everyone that the hunt was over when Bruce met Sherry.

Linda Falba

Bruce was my first boyfriend, and my crush on him lasted from the 4th through the 8th grade. I kept a diary when I was 13 and I think his name is on every page. I still have the diary.

He was a sweet guy and a cute guy. I remember he had this long neck and his head would just kind of bobble on it when he walked. He was a walking bobble-head doll. And you know the way kids play with their names, after a while Bruce Layne became Loose Brain, which was perfect for a guy with a bobble head. (He'll die when he reads all this….)

Anyway, I've stayed close to Bruce all through the years and he sometimes asks me, Why didn't we date later on, in high school? And I tell him, "We did have one date, Bruce."

It was when we were at Gorman, and it was in the spring, and we went to a drive-in movie. He had been to baseball practice that afternoon and was yawning through the first part of the movie. I had on a pink diamond argyle sweater, and as I was watching the movie and getting into it I suddenly noticed that Bruce had fallen asleep on my shoulder. But the worst part was that he had a string of drool going all the way down my beautiful sweater.

Supporters of Bob Miller

(Laughing loudly) I tell Bruce that is why we quit dating.

He was the kind of guy who would tell girls, "I'm harmless. I just want to cuddle," but I don't think any of us ever bought that line.

I remember once when a bunch of us, Bruce and Tommy Johnson and Katie Russo, I think, all told our parents we were staying with other friends for the night and we decided to go to the beach. Which in Las Vegas means driving to Los Angeles, a five-hour drive. Of course by the time we got there our time was up and we had to head home, so we just stuck our toes in the ocean and drove back. And none of us got caught, which is kind of amazing if you think about it.

A priest named Fr. McVeigh, who was our first pastor at St. Anne's grade school, has been at the center of our lives since we were children. We still have an annual retreat with him every June, and Bruce and Tito Tiberti and several others will come to San Francisco and we'll get together.

Bruce is very important to me. (Long pause as Linda collects herself.) He's always been behind me as a true friend, and he's one of those friends you can count on one hand that you could go to if you have a really serious problem. He's always been able to make me laugh and he laughs at all my jokes. It's priceless to have someone like that in your life.

A brilliant woman named Dr. Emmy Werner has written a book on resiliency, and she says there are four factors that make a person resilient: 1) social competence; 2) an ability to isolate from dysfunction in your own family; 3) a sense of your own future; 4) an ability to solve problems.

If you think about this, Bruce has all four of these qualities. He was able to separate himself from some of the problems in his own family growing up and say, "Okay, my family may not be getting along too well, but that doesn't have to stop me from having a successful life." And he's always been a romantic, full of the possibilities and the great things that can happen if you charge ahead. And he's certainly a problem solver. And finally, everyone likes him. He epitomizes social competence. So when you look at the positive way he's approaching his current challenges with Parkinson's, he really defines what resiliency is all about.

I'm just so happy that he's been my friend my whole life.

Dennis Finfrock

Bruce and I were diagnosed with Parkinson's a couple years apart, so we both landed in the soup at about the same time. In 1997 I opted to have a Pallidotomy, which is an operation in which a part of the globus pallidus section of the brain is destroyed. During the operation the patient is awake, with an 11-inch probe inside the brain. It's pretty wild. I had it done by Dr. Robert Iacono of Loma Linda, and it was a tremendous success. Ever since then my left side has been steady as a rock. Anyway, I've shared information with Bruce all along the way, and while I knew him before we had our diagnoses, I think we're much closer now that we have this shared challenge.

Bruce stays in really good spirits nearly all the time, and I think when we talk or see each other we do each other some good. We can laugh about it together, but more importantly we can cry about it together.

I think his financial success has freed him from some of the worries I have, and that is being able to generate anything near the income level I had when I was at UNLV (as interim athletic director and also head of the Thomas and Mack Center) and later at the MGM Grand. I'm fortunate right now to be working with some great guys at the Rampart Casino.

I feel that my Parkinson's is connected to all the stress I was under during the years of upheaval at UNLV, with the basketball scandals and all the depositions I had to give. I spent about four years with all of that. I could never get it off my mind because I always had a deposition coming up in two or three months and had to prepare for those. But Bruce and I will work together on a steering committee in Las Vegas to generate support of those with Parkinson's, and that will be a rewarding experience.

One positive spin I can put on it is that, as an avid fly fisherman, having a right arm that shakes makes my fly on the water looks like it's dancing, and that attracts the fish. How's that for turning lemons into lemonade?

Ken Fleming
(A letter in response to Bruce's failed bid for Lieutenant Governor)

Politics is the real world turned upside down. Illusion means more than reality, name recognition is more valuable than reputation, and absolute values are detrimental as they provide definitive targets. In politics, cream sinks to the bottom and gold floats to the top. Also, there is no penalty for lying.

Lies are often rewarded, as in the case of Bill and Hillary. They told people their health plan would provide universal coverage at no additional cost and that they would champion a middle-class tax cut. Clinton was elected although he had no tax plan, and then he raised taxes on everyone.

Politicians get elected by promising social benefits that taxpaying voters are unwilling to pay for. They create obscene debt, exempt themselves from the inane laws they pass, and dance around truth with half-lies and almost denials.

Congratulations on not dropping into the cesspool of derogatory campaigning. Your focus on personal endorsements and past community contributions was mature and appropriate.

89

Hammargren's half-truth about the Massimino vote was much more successful, but that's politics.

I admire and support you as a human being. You are a good friend and a poor politician. Those are two very fine attributes.

John Glenn

How could I ever forget, among the many great times I've had with Bruce, our salmon fishing trips to Alaska? Being in the wild with a guy who's never out of a four-star hotel is quite an experience.

The first year I made all the reservations, and so of course, when we got to the lodge, all the experienced help had quit and it was a mess. And Bruce had to walk barefoot on wet, grimy floors to get to a wet, grimy bathroom each night. He was groaning about it, so after a couple days I said, "So, why don't you put on shoes?"

But with all the inconvenience, Bruce was still a real trooper. He had preached to me about the importance of taking your kids individually on a trip each year, and my son J.P. was with us that year. And Bruce saw that as an opportunity to really mentor J.P., who was 16 at the time, and get him re-motivated for school. That just seemed like Bruce's top priority on that trip, to connect with my son and give him good advice.

Another time we ran out of booze, and so of course we had to hire our guide's wife to fly back to Anchorage and buy more vodka at about a hundred bucks a bottle plus tip, and of course get some Gran Marnier for Leo Seevers. God knows Leo was not going to make it in the wild without his Gran Marnier.

The Indian chief's son, a Tyonek Indian with a long ponytail, told us he liked to come to Las Vegas and gamble a little and hang out at the strip clubs, so of course Bruce made it a point to hang out with him the next time he was in town. You talk about a people person: Bruce was more than happy to hang with a guy he'd met just once or twice, let alone the guy who had kept a grizzly bear from eating him. It was almost like he was an ambassador for Las Vegas in the same way that the guide had shown us around the Alaskan wilderness.

That old expression "life was made not for living, but for giving," really applies to my friend Bruce. He just shows so much concern and respect for people that you've got to love him.

And here I told myself that I wasn't going to be obsequious in this testimonial to Bruce, but what are you gonna do?

Glenn Hall

I met Bruce at Layne & Associates in 1997, when I worked there on a monthly basis doing chair massage for his employees. Although our first contact was a business one, we became friends. The environment in Bruce's office was always one that was very pleasant to be around.

I found Bruce to be an incredibly creative person who enjoyed life and humor as much as anyone I have ever known. He has a wonderful sense of humor that shows in all he does.

Just working around Bruce tends to make you more aware of your surroundings and what is being offered to you. There is a lot more beauty and respect than most people are aware of. Bruce makes the working environment pleasant, something not many business owners are capable of doing.

In 1998 I noted that he appeared to be stooping forward a little bit and that his posture seemed different. I had, once before, recommended that he see a doctor after a massage session. That time it was kidney stones. It would be a little while before I would learn that the change in his posture was caused by Parkinson's Disease.

Once he was diagnosed, he was very open about it. It seemed odd to me that his staff tended to be very quiet about it, as if to protect him. Few people could make such a finding about how their life was about to change — and not for the positive healthwise — and turn it around into a positive experience.

But Bruce did.

Mary Hamilton

I have cut Bruce and Sherry's hair for nearly 20 years. Their son Trevor and my son Paul were friends in high school, and Bruce was nice enough to give Paul his first job.

Bruce is far more than just my client. He is my friend and mentor and just a wonderful person. I can't think of a bad time we've ever had together. I always look forward to seeing him.

I wish I knew where Bruce gets his inner drive. Maybe it's natural curiosity, or just the need and desire to grow and expand, but I know I've been inspired by him since we first met.

The best things in life are good health and good friends. I just feel blessed to have Bruce in my life.

Paul Hamilton

I was having a rough time in my early years of college. I was a bit of a handful and I had moments where I felt that no one could really understand what I was going through. But Bruce changed all that. He told me he had also lacked direction at my age, but finally found his purpose.

One story that has really stayed with me occurred one morning when I stopped by Bruce's office unannounced, seeking advice. The reception area was full of businessmen in suits, antsy to get in to see him. I was starting to turn around and get back on the elevator, realizing that this was not a good time, when he came out and saw me there. Bruce almost looked right through these gentlemen

and told them he'd be with them as soon as his appointment with me was over. I was just amazed that he would squeeze me in like that, knowing I hadn't called beforehand. But that isn't all. I felt rushed to explain why I was there with all the people waiting, but Bruce said to just calm down and forget about them. He ended up speaking with me for well over a half-hour.

The bottom line is that when you are around Bruce he makes you feel like the most important person in the world, and he sincerely cares what you are talking to him about.

I am now a mortgage banker. I loan private funds on behalf of my clients and secure their money with real estate. I had trained diligently and buried myself in learning the business from top to bottom. Bruce continued to encourage me in my endeavors through these years. As I was training, I was asking a list of friends and contacts if they'd invest in my deals when I was ready. I believe I had a list of 87 contacts who had said, "absolutely," or "I can't wait."

When the time came, however, I received 86 phenomenal excuses as to why they could not invest, and only one "absolutely." As you might have guessed, the one person who was good to his promise was Bruce Layne.

Mike Hastings

While Bruce was a heck of an athlete in high school: a good football player and a great baseball player, basketball was not his best sport. He was on the team his junior and senior years at Gorman, when we won state championships both seasons, but he was never a starter.

Despite that, he worked harder than anyone on the team in practice. The coach usually had him guarding me in practice because he knew Bruce would push me as hard as I could be pushed. It's not easy, when you excel in two different sports, to be relegated to the bench, but I never once in those years heard Bruce complain about not getting to play.

After being sort of a local hero, if you will, in high school, I went on to St. Louis University to play basketball, and in my years on the varsity I found that there wasn't a lot of use for a six-foot forward at the major college level. It was extremely disheartening. I thought several times about transferring back home to the Las Vegas area and playing at a smaller school, but whenever I would get down, I would realize I was in the position that Bruce had been in at Gorman. That kept me from giving up, and it kept me working hard to do the best I could. I used my memory of what Bruce had done in high school basketball and it inspired me to keep a good attitude.

I've learned to appreciate Bruce even more through the years, watching him grow his business and maintain a great family life. The guy is just relentlessly positive, and a terrific friend. And I can't thank him enough for being such an inspiration to me.

R. J. Heher

There are a couple of things about Bruce that I recall vividly. One is that, while he was a strong, athletic guy in high school, more than capable of taking care of himself in a fight, I don't remember his ever getting into one. He avoided fights and used diplomacy instead. He was just such a solid guy, so balanced in his life and positive in his outlook, that he probably understood at an age when most kids don't that fighting was pretty senseless, and that these brawls usually started over nothing more important than whose chip was on whose shoulder.

Bruce always gave me the impression of knowing exactly what he wanted from life, and he was clever about how he went about getting it.

He was so charming and tactful he gave me the impression of being the type of guy who was smiling at you while he was eating your lunch. I always admired that about him.

I also recall that, when he would come to our house for dinner, he was the only one among my friends who would take the time to engage my grandmother in conversation. She was about 90 years old at the time, and it wasn't uncommon for people to ignore her or just treat her like she was part of the furniture. But Bruce would always visit with her and seem genuinely concerned about her. And Grandma always got excited when she heard Bruce was coming by because he treated her like a human being.

I also once was at a drive-in movie and I looked over and in the next car was Bruce and his date, and his kid brother Timmy in the back seat. He took on the responsibility of taking care of that boy, but he never let that obligation affect his positive outlook. I even remember his taking the kid to parties and including him in every activity. That's pretty remarkable, for a teenager to be that responsible and considerate.

Phil Hernandez

It's been my pleasure to work with Bruce as his personal shopper for about 14 years, and in that time our relationship has grown into a nice friendship. Bruce is one of a group of his friends, including Tito Tiberti, John Glenn, and Steve Ducharme, who are distinguished businessmen, and I think they all keep one another on their toes and looking good. These men all know how to dress with elegance and style.

I appreciate that Bruce relies on my taste in suits, sport coats, and ties, and he trusts my judgment when it comes to selecting business gifts or personal gifts to friends. He is extremely funny and easy to work with, and we always have good laughs whenever he comes by Neiman Marcus.

Clyde Horner

I first met Bruce in the early 1980s when I was a CFO and he was growing his insurance agency. I was the typical finance person, seeing things in black and white and with a conservative view, and Bruce was just the opposite, entrepreneurial and always optimistic. This difference in our personalities caused me to miss out on getting to know Bruce as a person and seeing what he offered, namely integrity and care for others. My focus on details and results blinded me to Bruce's approach, which was much more people-oriented. Consequently, I was never open to Bruce's ideas, and I told him that directly.

To my surprise and amazement, Bruce never held that against me, although he certainly remembered our conflict. Twenty years later, he is able to put that behind him, and he is very supportive. This shows a great deal of forgiveness and integrity. During the one-to-one time I've spent with him, he has been patient with my probing and nudging, and has always given me positive feedback.

Bruce exhibits behavior that sets a great example for others. Our relationship started with a lack of understanding, was interrupted by a long silence, and yet has continued and thrived because Bruce has shown compassion and leadership values that are worthy for others to follow. I am very appreciative!

Richard Kumler

In 1985 I was an underwriting manager for an insurance company in Newport Beach. One day I received a call from Bruce asking me to write the insurance policies for the Dunes and Maxim casinos, which were owned by a California farmer named John Anderson.

In 1994 I was basically "on the street," and Bruce took me in and let me start over in insurance.

He gave me back my life, in more ways than just this one.

The best time — even though it doesn't sound like something good — was when Bruce came to talk to me. He said, "You're getting to be a fat boy. You need to join a gym and work out." Not only did I do that, but he even paid for it. During that time, I managed to injure my shoulder enough to require an x-ray. The shoulder turned out to be okay, but — the big but — they saw something in one of my lungs, and after a few more x-rays I found out that I had lung cancer and that my time on this earth was rapidly coming to a halt. After five surgeries and a lot of radiation therapy, I'm still here. If Bruce hadn't told me I was getting too fat and needed to work it off, I wouldn't be here today. He saved my life.

Kevin Lay

I had known Bruce from when I was an underwriter, and I'd done some business with him when I was living in Arizona. I knew from looking at his company in about 1990 that he was doing more business than anyone in Las Vegas. I found out right away that his word was good as gold. He was ethical and totally honest and pulled no punches.

In 1998 Jim Harris sold his company to Brown and Brown, and I was brought to Las Vegas to run the office for them. I knew at the time that Bruce had spoken to Marsh and McClellan about selling Layne & Associates, and about a month after I got here I discussed the possibility of his looking at our company. The only thing that seemed to be in the way of that's happening was a pending litigation with Mandalay Bay.

He could easily have taken the simple route with Mandalay and gotten them to agree to a deal that would allow the sale to Brown and Brown to go through. He could have agreed to testify in the case to anything Mandalay Bay wanted him to say, just so that it wouldn't impede the sale of his company — and we're talking about millions of dollars going into Bruce's pocket — but through the entire process Bruce handled the situation with class. He always took the high road, and he eventually got Mandalay Bay to cap the liability at $6 million, which allowed his company to be sold to ours.

The impressive thing is that he never took the easy path. He handled the entire situation with class, and that's what sets him apart from ordinary people. We're very pleased with the results of the takeover. I'd always felt that his company's entrepreneurial spirit and the way they took care of their clients made them a perfect fit for our company, and that's the way it's worked out.

Francis Lynch

I got to know Bruce over 20 years ago when I was an executive with Boyd Gaming. I was researching property and casualty insurance and came in contact with him. I found him to be a real square shooter who was able to answer all my questions. It was important to me to meet the insurers directly because these were very large policies; I traveled to San Francisco and Los Angeles with him and found him to be a delightful fellow.

I know that he's one of the few businessmen in town who's actually a native of Las Vegas, and I also know he had some tough years growing up. Many of his friends were from wealthy families, which wasn't the case with him, so his success is very hard earned and deserved.

From what I've seen he's waging a good fight against Parkinson's, staying in shape and keeping a good frame of mind. I'm honored to contribute to his memoirs because he's a good man. One quick anecdote that makes me laugh: when I met his mother-in-law at a social function she told me, "I never thought he would amount to anything." Well, he proved her wrong.

Bob Mayer

In a town built on fantasies of lust and greed, Bruce Layne succeeded while having a life based on principles, ethics, spirituality, and integrity. I am proud to call him my friend.

Margy McGonagill

My relationship with Bruce Layne began when he met my very special sister-in-law, Sherry. My affection for Bruce grew stronger as together we faced the challenges from our mutual mother-in-law — neither of us was good enough. These early years established a bond that has remained for over 30 years.

Although I left Las Vegas in 1973, I have remained in touch with Sherry, Bruce, my godson Chad, and Trevor, This strong connection is due in large part to Sherry and Bruce's efforts to include me as part of their family.

I watched with pride from a distance as the entire family grew. Chad and Trevor's growing into manhood; Sherry's getting involved in literacy and education through the library board and finally pursuing her life-long love of horses; Bruce's expanding his accomplishments as a businessman, as well as his role as a community leader. Though physically apart, Sherry and I are like sisters, and Bruce and I still consider ourselves comrades.

Bruce and I share a new bond now. We are woven together by Bruce's Parkinson's and my interest in furthering Parkinson's research. I became involved as an advocate for increased federal funding for the disease and a volunteer in the Tucson chapter of the American Parkinson's Disease by the news Association before I learned of Bruce's diagnosis. I was stunned by the news, but it has served to personalize my efforts in a dramatic way.

Bob Miller

Bruce and I have been friends since the fifth grade, and he is one of my two or three closest friends in life. Our mothers were friendly and were the core of our two families, and we were classmates who played sports and chased girls together growing up. I'll admit he was a better athlete and always did better with the girls.

Bruce had to scrounge a lot as a kid. When his parents divorced and his older brother had some problems he had to grow up pretty fast, and I know it was a difficult period for him. A pivotal time for him was when he went to UNLV on a baseball scholarship and flunked out his first year. He was forced to take a job in a titanium plant in Henderson, and

that was a dose of reality for him. He wanted to keep pace with his friends and pursue a good career, and before long he was back at UNLV and doing well on the baseball team. As I recall he batted about .395 one year.

After college he married Sherry and moved to L.A. to learn the insurance business with Marsh and McLennan, and then later with Cash, Sullivan, and Cross. He just excelled at the insurance profession. I thought it was amazing that, starting with nothing, he was able by the early 1980s to create or locate enough capital to buy the business. That was a magnificent feat. Bruce's success has always come from his own natural gregariousness and

The last night at the Govenor's Mansion, Bob and Sandy, Bruce and Sherry, Tito and Sandy

trustworthiness. People like him immediately and sense that he is totally honest.

When he ran for lieutenant governor, I think he was at a point in life where he'd accomplished a lot in business and was looking in other directions for ways to contribute. It's too bad that whole experience didn't work out for him, because he would have made a great lieutenant governor.

The first inklings that he had this condition that was later diagnosed as Parkinson's occurred on our annual getaway. That year we were in Sao Paolo, Brazil with Tito Tiberti. Bruce was mugged while walking down the street. We knew that he had been moving more slowly, but that incident seemed to magnify everything. It's bothered me ever since Bruce was diagnosed that I didn't pick up on it sooner, but it was a gradual thing, and maybe if I hadn't seen him as often as I did it would have been more dramatic to observe.

I'm surprised that anyone could remain this upbeat in the face of Parkinson's. But Bruce has always been a very positive, forward-looking person. That's just one of his many strong character traits and another reason he's such a great friend.

Brad Mishlove

Bruce is successful for a myriad of reasons. He is motivated, interested in people, and compassionate. He brings a level of caring for people that warms the heart, and he devotes his time and energy to bettering our community. He just has that passion — that fire in the belly — that brings positive results to those around him.

Bruce understands the sales process and its critical role in business success, and he is instinctively aware of the risks and rewards of business ownership, He also has the ability to interpret keenly the value in any business situation.

I am proud to call him my friend.

Pam Newell

Over the years, I have been fortunate enough to get to know Bruce as a loving family man, an astute business person, a wise mentor, a sincere guidance counselor, and most of all, a precious friend. It is amazing how one person like Bruce Layne can positively impact the lives of so many people. Bruce's passion and enthusiasm for life is contagious. His good will has spread across the state of Nevada and far beyond its borders. Bruce has truly made the world a better place. He has greatly enhanced my life just by my knowing him.

Bruce Layne has the gift of being able to scratch through the superficial and communicate with people on a deeper level. Although Parkinson's has created many challenges for him, Bruce has embraced the opportunity to reach out to so many people that are coping with the disease and really need his help and inspiration. Bruce is a wonderful example of caring, compassion, and kindness.

Last, but certainly not least, Bruce Layne is my hero! Webster's describes "hero" as "a man of distinguished valor or fortitude: a man admired for his noble deeds or qualities." That's Bruce Layne!

Stephen Pearne

I have now known Bruce for more than half my life. I will never forget the start of our friendship in October, 1970. I had just arrived in Los Angeles as a mid-twenties Englishman to start a two-year contract in the same insurance brokerage as Bruce. Bruce was one of the first people I met, not just in the company, but in America. As excited as I was to be in America, I took a surprisingly long time to settle and adjust to my new surroundings and lifestyle, as part of me wanted to be back in England. This is where I first experienced Bruce's kind and sympathetic counseling skills. These, together with many hours, drinks, and hamburgers with him and Sherry, brought me the perspective I needed to make a smooth transition to my new life in the USA, and I have never looked back.

He would often call me "the dumb Limey," but in a most affectionate way. He still calls me that today, so what does that tell you about his teaching skills?

To help further my adjustment to the "American Way," as I was on my own he invited me to spend my first Christmas in the USA with him and Sherry in Las Vegas. This was another gesture of his kindness and hospitality. I had a really enjoyable time with them that Christmas, and still remember how different Christmas in Las Vegas was from the traditional Christmas back in "jolly old" England.

Bruce also taught me how to adapt to American dining. Hamburgers in England in 1970 were a mere fraction of the size of American hamburgers. In those days McDonald's had not discovered the "colonies," despite selling enough of them to reach the moon and halfway back. When presented with my first quarter-pounder with everything on it, I had no idea how I was going to eat it. Bruce stepped in to show me the art of eating them, and I am now an old pro!

It is such a pleasure and privilege to have Bruce as a good friend. We only see each other maybe once a year when I return to the USA on a business trip, or when he and Sherry have stayed at my home in England. These visits are all too short, but I always look forward to being with them again. I have enjoyed following Bruce's life and career and the well deserved success that he has achieved.

Bruce always has time for people, whether they are his family, employees, friends, or passing acquaintances. Whenever we are in a restaurant or at his golf club or in a store, people from the owner to the waitresses and busboys will come up and say hello. He always has time for them all, and he makes them feel special. There are very few people I know that have his genuine warmth and friendly personality and his desire to help others, especially young people. I have seen him in action at UNLV, teaching students about how to achieve success and defining what success really means. I certainly learned that success is not always a new Mercedes on the drive.

Marc Ratner

Bruce was the first extremely business-oriented member we'd had on the Nevada Athletic Commission. One important contribution he made was redesigning the promoter's application so that promoters would be more accountable. This new application is more in line with the application to have a gaming license, and we still use it today.

I think Bruce really enjoyed being on the Commission, and I was sorry to see him leave when he made the decision to run for Lieutenant Governor. In hindsight, I wish he would have taken a leave of absence from the Commission rather than resigning from it.

Bruce is also responsible for the rule that the cage at the casino or hotel hosting a fight be provided with enough cash by the promoter so that the fighters can cash their checks there. He was always looking out for the little guy on the under card of a big fight who might be in there battling for $400 or $600.

I do have a memory of Bruce's having to tell Tony Tubbs that he had failed a drug test because of cocaine in his system. There are unpleasant things that have to be done from time to time on the Commission, and Bruce was more than willing to do those.

My memories of Bruce actually precede his time on the Commission. I went to Las Vegas High School at about the same time as he went to Gorman, and I remember him as a good athlete, as a good hitting first baseman both at Gorman and at Nevada Southern.

Timbuck Moore Rivera

I remember that in grade school Bruce Layne was just the cutest guy there was. He and Tommy Johnson and Tito Tiberti were the popular guys that all the girls swooned over. And being totally honest about it, I was considered a scag. That was actually the word they used back then, and I couldn't deny it. I was slow developing and not very pretty, and I didn't become a "hottie" until later on. So of course Bruce was out of my league as a boyfriend, but I thought about him a lot.

Anyway, this one day in seventh grade at St. Anne's the boys were acting stupid and throwing rocks in our direction to show off, and as bad luck would have it Bruce threw one that hit Vicki Moler in the face. It broke her glasses and actually put glass in her eye. She wore a patch for weeks afterward. Well, Bruce was horrified by what he'd done, and although Vicki was the kind of girl he wouldn't have given the time of day to prior to that event, he fawned over her like crazy for months afterward. He just did everything he could for her, partly to absolve the guilt and because he felt so badly.

What I remember most vividly was that I was tremendously jealous of Vicki during that time, having this cute guy bend over backwards for her, to the point that I wished I had been the one who'd been hit by the rock. Now there's a story I'll bet no one else remembered!

Barbara Saccamano

I first met Bruce in March of 1994; the human resources manager at Layne & Associates hired me for a position in the mail room. Bruce used to come by the mail room and stop in just to say hi and pick up his mail, or he would come in and ask me to make copies for him. I knew after just a few weeks this was the perfect place to work. It was like being at home with your family, and even though

mine was the lowest position there, I was still happy and content.

After my first year I was promoted from the mail room to be Bruce's assistant. I was really nervous about taking the position, but being assistant to the president of the company might be a one-time opportunity for me. I explained to Bruce that I did not have much experience in the insurance field, but he was very positive and said it was okay, that I could learn, and that he had confidence in me. He said there were all kinds of courses I could take, and that the company pays for you to educate yourself. And he was right!

Over the years I could feel myself becoming attached to him. We worked together closely on a daily basis, whether it was insurance or his personal schedule. He taught me how to set goals and achieve them. He always had an open door policy, and you could go in and talk to him about anything.

Bruce's success is amazing, and I respect it. I think this is a gift and he has a special guardian angel with him because of his beliefs and his good nature. Maybe it is his Grandma Mimi? The Vegas luck just went with it, due to his community involvement and caring and giving to this state. I think this Parkinson's is just another test that God has given him to conquer!

Bruce has always been a firm believer in education and providing career paths for students. In April of 2002, at our 5th annual career day breakfast, Bruce was introduced to a group of 200 senior students and 100 teachers. As he started his speech on careers and goals that inspire students to achieve, his first sentence was: "Last year I was diagnosed with the same thing that Michael J. Fox and Muhammad Ali have." My heart started to flutter and my eyes filled with tears and all I could think was, "You go, Layne!" Acceptance of this disease has to be one of the hardest things in life to do. But like Bruce always said to me, "CHANGE

IS GOOD!" Whether it be for the bad or good, he always accepts what is put on his plate (even if it's pumpkin raviolis) and deals with it. He has now started a Nevada Parkinson's Board in Nevada to educate and help people with Parkinson's who live in Nevada. I attended the first meeting so that I can help him and other people. I know this is a goal of his and that he will be successful, and I intend to help him along the way. I have never really volunteered for anything like this before, and I feel really good about it. This is just another good quality that Bruce has brought out in me.

This past year, after the sale of his company, Bruce took me and another co-worker to Italy. I had the best time ever! This was a chance of a lifetime for me and I was very grateful for it, even though I tried to cash my ticket in several times. We laughed so hard in the back of cab rides wondering if we were ever going to get out of the cab alive: they don't have the best driving roads or skills over there. The bathrooms were hysterical. Any time we needed to use the rest room, we would look at each other and say, "You go first so you can let me know what to expect." The worst was in Pisa. You had to pay one Euro to use the rest room. The attendant would let you in. I was behind Bruce, so she let me into a room and it was not a toilet! When I opened the door to leave, I was in the men's room. I screamed for Bruce, and he was laughing. Good thing they didn't understand English. When we viewed the leaning tower of Pisa there was a chain rope all around it and over the chain was a sign, but in order to read it you had to step over the chain and walk up to it. The sign read, "Do not walk on the grass." He called us over and said, "Hey, come here! You have to see this," and we climbed over the chain and walked up to the sign and just cracked up laughing. Like, maybe they should have the sign in front of the chain? This was definitely an adventure and great experience for me, and I couldn't think of another person I would have wanted to be with.

Tom Schoeman

My first recollections of Bruce are not of Bruce himself, but of Layne & Associates. His firm's reputation for integrity and providing high-quality service preceded our introduction. I provided some modest support for Bruce when he ran for public office, and he tells me I was one of a very select few.

I believe the true character of a person is revealed in the face of adversity. Bruce has confronted Parkinson's disease not just with a passion for life, but a passion for improving the community of people afflicted with this illness. I applaud and admire him for his efforts and support him in his search for as many 10's as possible.

Roger Scullion

The insurance business works in cycles and is normally tied into the stock market. When an insurance company can make more money by investing in the stock market, underwriting for a profit becomes a secondary issue: they want as much premium on the books as they can possibly get. This is when the "Deals" get made. We insurance professionals call this cycle "The Soft Market."

When I first met Bruce in 1985, the "Soft Market" had hardened overnight. We insurance professionals call this the "Hard Market." (You can actually go to school to learn how to do this stuff.) Everyone was trying to take advantage of everyone else. Bruce, however, fought long and hard for his clients and still tried to make the best deals for them without compromising his own very strong belief in what is right and what is wrong. I like to say that Bruce put the "grit" in "integrity."

The first client we worked on together was the Boyd Group, who had a watercraft problem in Laughlin. Together, Bruce and I changed their program so that they were not being penalized by an insurance company's inability to write the small ferry boats that went between the various casinos. It saved them a bundle.

99

At this point I started coming to Las Vegas to meet with Bruce and his staff, and got to know Bruce on a personal level. I'll never forget the first time we all went to lunch. When the meals finally arrived at the table, Bruce was looking at all the various choices displayed in front of him and requested a taste of each — especially dessert! He knows how to have fun. If you don't have a sense of humor, don't apply! We have spent many an evening doubled over with laughter, telling silly stories and, in some cases, acting them out. I've often thought about getting Bruce a cape or a cloak. You know, "Bruce Layne, Boxing Commissioner," Batman type of thing. But Bruce is not a Batman type. He's more like the mild mannered Clark Kent who disappears into a phone booth and emerges ready to do battle with the enemies of mankind, except Bruce disappears into his office. Then, suddenly, the mild mannered Bruce Layne vanishes and "Insurance Man" reaches out for his instrument of power, the telephone, and the saga begins. Bruce fights for his clients, each and every one of them.

Bruce seems to have the ability to break everything down to the lowest common denominator. He can get to the root of a problem and (usually) solve it without making mortal enemies of the participants. This is a true gift.

Everyone else that I know of who has made his or her "To Hell with you money" has disappeared into the woodwork. Bruce could have done that years ago, but he chose a higher path. He spent a fortune on the political front. It didn't work, and the cost of that experience would have made a lot of other people very bitter. Not Bruce. He continued on with his core beliefs. (This does not make him a saint. He is a Catholic, but he is not a saint. Even he will tell you that.) Bruce enjoys his life. That sounds corny, but listen to him talk! He talks with passion, conviction, and reason (he should have been a Democrat). He cares about what goes on around him. He makes a difference.

Many people have underestimated Bruce. I hope that many more do the same.

Leo Seevers

One of my most memorable moments with Bruce occurred in the summer of 2001 when we went on a salmon fishing trip to Alaska. Out in the wilds of that country we had to wear a lot of clothing and equipment before going on the boat each morning; preparing for the daily excursion was akin to a knight's putting on his armor before battle.

Recognizing that this was going to be a challenge for Bruce, without even thinking twice Chad and Trevor jumped right in and volunteered to help their dad get ready, hoping to make it easier for him. It was an instinctive act of love and consideration on their parts, and it happened so naturally that I actually found myself getting emotional watching them.

It recalled for me how the previous year, on our group trip to Hawaii, when I would turn on the TV in the morning it would always be on either MTV or the World Wrestling Federation channel. And that's because as a concession to his sons, Bruce would watch that stuff with them in the evenings, although I'm quite certain those shows would not have been his first choice;

This selfless, unconditional love that exists between Bruce and his sons is something I'll never forget.

Sherman Simmons

My first memories of Bruce date back to when we were in the 8th grade. I went to Fremont Jr. High and he went to Saint Anne's. We played Pop Warner football together for a team called the Wranglers, coached by Bob Brunier. We practiced and played at Saint Anne's playground field and the circle park on Maryland Parkway. The next year we were freshmen at Bishop Gorman High School, and Bruce lived near downtown, near 8th and Budger.

He was one of the cool guys in high school, a fellow member of the Sirs Social Club as well as varsity athlete on several high school teams.

When many of the fellow students went away to college, Bruce stayed in Las Vegas attending UNLV, then called NSU (Nevada Southern University). After college he entered the insurance business, and the rest is history. He developed the

company into one of the premier players in our state.

Bruce continued to be active in sports, playing tennis at a competitive level. At the same time, he was a fine father to his two sons who are now grown and successful businessmen, one having blessed him with healthy, beautiful grandchildren.

Bruce has been a world-class facilitator; it comes naturally to him. When he was in YPO (Young Presidents' Organization) he was very active in the education processes, the forum experience as well as the social side. He has continued to spearhead the forum-type experience with many of the past members and his friends throughout the years. He continues to be very reflective about the meanings of life, including its spirituality and the importance of our short time here.

He is a very centered individual. When he was diagnosed with Parkinson's disease, in addition to being somewhat of a setback it was disorienting and confusing, but I think he was able to see through it, or past its initial impact on his life, to a deeper importance and passion for life. Being the fierce competitor that he has been has given him a quiet strength. He has been his own best competition, always trying to improve not

Sherman, Susan, and Tito **101**

only himself, but others he's with. Bruce is very open-minded and accepting, trustworthy and trusting. He is desirous of exploring new ideas and worlds that are different. He is compassionate, generous, humorous, and respectful. His energy and enthusiasm are contagious. He is an original, a winner, and we **all** love him.

Susan DiBiase Simmons

This past summer when I walked into Bruce's office to discuss insurance and also hoping for help with my life's problems, little did I know it would be the beginning of a true friendship.

In the course our conversation as my problems, slowly at first, came, tumbling out, I had hopes that providence had guided me to him. Little did I know then that he had the gift of guidance, of helping others find their paths again. For months before that visit last summer I had been praying for guidance. So many decisions had been weighing on my mind — too many in hindsight. Now I know that I was depressed. Crying in church was a given, or when I heard beautiful music, or thought about my loved ones. In fact, hardly a day went by without crying. I had hit bottom and knew it. That was when I really prayed. I knew I could no longer carry the weight of my problems by myself. One night I asked God to take my problems.

I continued to pray, every morning and at night. I also thought a lot in every quiet moment I had. It became clear to me that God was guiding me from above, but I also needed real friends down here on Earth. Whom did I have? Who could understand my problems? To whom could I turn for answers? After a great deal of thought I decided I would turn to Bruce. My reasoning told me that he is a good person, someone I can trust and someone who has been through similar difficulties. So off I headed to his office for help.

As he listened, quite intently, I noticed that he seemed to understand everything I was saying. He did not pity me or even side with me, but instead urged me forward with well-directed discipline and criticism. He challenged me to question the way I was thinking, not giving me the answers, but leading me to them. He even gave me homework (like this assignment) that would open up my closed mind so that I could "see" or understand things from different perspectives. What a gift! That first day, after much crying, I walked out of his office knowing God had led me there, knowing I was with the right person for the help I needed. I looked forward anxiously to another visit the following week, after I had done my homework.

Now, months later, I see a problem as a challenge, nothing more. With time they can all be worked out, and things do work out for the best. I believe that.

Dad said to me one day, "You know, for every positive there is a negative." After some reflection I said to him, "Then for every negative there must be a positive." I knew then that I had won! Now, that is how I look at difficulties: where is the positive? How many positives?

After many months I remember saying to Bruce, "I hope I can help others, giving back the way you have been able to help me." If I can pass it along by helping someone else out of their hole, then I will know satisfaction, the real spirit of giving.

That is what Bruce has: the real and beautiful spirit of giving. He is a real "doctor of the spirit."

My wish for Bruce? May God continue to keep him in all ways, in all of the work of his life's path. And may his work light the path for many, many others, until the end of time.

Monte Smith

One day in July, 1986, Bruce received a phone call from the Risk Manager of Summa Corporation. At that time, Summa was at its pinnacle and had a division that owned numerous large hotel casinos on the Las Vegas Strip. The Risk Manager announced to Bruce that he was interested in hiring me, but wanted first to let Bruce know of his intent. I didn't know any of this, as I was out of town. When I made a regular call in at end of day after class, Bruce said that he must speak with me. He then relayed the story and explained that this could be a good opportunity for me; I should carefully consider it. In this long distance telephone call Bruce showed support and concern for my future. I think I was a little in shock over the initial offer, and Bruce was being so objective and so supportive that I was taken aback. I remember I thought he was being a little too supportive and too objective, and asked him point blank, "Are you trying to get rid of me?"

When I got back to Las Vegas, we went through an exercise that is signature Bruce Layne — the "T Chart." One side lists "pros" and one "con's," including weighting the issues. We both knew I had a promising future with Layne & Associates and, we set some high expectations from Summa. At the end of numerous discussions, we had established terms that would make the move a good one. As it turned out, the terms that were offered didn't pass my criteria. And, the results in the months and years following demonstrated that the terms we set were right on. At this writing, I have just had an anniversary, 26 years working with Bruce Layne — I think this shows that, with his help, I was led to make the right decision. My point is, at that moment in 1986 it was a terrifically important and difficult decision. The answer at first was not clear at all. The offer was most flattering and could have been easy to jump at. It was through Bruce's thoughtful and caring guidance that we saw this through together. I think this process and outcome is most unusual between employer and employee.

In all these years, I've observed so many instances where Bruce interacts with others to help them make right decisions.

Craig F. Sullivan

I met Bruce Layne in April, 1995. I was the new CFO of Primadonna Resorts and Bill Paulos foisted the insurance peddler off on me to "hear his spiel."

At the time, I was in over my head. A bridge loan was past due to FIBN. The company's entire capital structure was in limbo. NY-NY financing was delayed and counter to PRMA's proposed capital structure. The company had no systems, policies, programs, or procedures. We were a mess. I was under pressure; I was intense. I was working 80-hour weeks. Insurance was number 157 on my priority list. Into this situation walked Bruce Layne.

Engaging, laid back, taking his time, he just wanted to chat — to get to know one another. I needed this schlemiel like an earache at a ski resort.

It turned out we were neighbors at Quail Ridge Estates. He knew everyone in town. I was a newcomer. He sized up my stressed out situation perfectly. He was straightforward beyond belief, telling a "new kid" whom he could trust and whom not to trust at the highest levels I would be dealing with both at my company and in town. I didn't have five minutes for him. He stayed two hours. Upon departure, he was the best new friend I had made in Las Vegas. Seven and a half years later, he's still my best new friend in Las Vegas.

We both have friends of long standing. It's unusual to make that close a friend this late in life, particularly if it hasn't been developed through business. Although women are usually better at sizing up people than I, Bruce has a keen "woman's intuition" about people. He is a superb judge of character. Bruce is one of the wisest, most

103

insightful people I've ever met. He's sincere in his charm, he's generous — not just with family and friends — but with everybody. He's fair. He's got a good heart. He's spiritual, if not religious. He's a good friend to a lot of people, and you can count on him to be there if you need him,

It would be inappropriate to recite the Boy Scout oath because I suspect he hasn't always been a Boy Scout. But if you need a "fox hole friend" you can count on with warmth and integrity, Bruce is your man. And he sells insurance! Can you believe it! He'd better be careful — he could give insurance salesmen a good name.

Roger Tabor

I have always considered Bruce my mentor. For the past 16 years, he has exhibited an understanding of me and my particular challenges, even when I wasn't aware of them myself. I have often solicited his advice, and in most cases followed it.

As I started writing this letter, however, it occurred to me you that he is more than a mentor. Bruce is my friend. True friendships are the most valuable assets a person can have. I will always be grateful for the quality time he has shared so generously with me. My only hope is that our friendship has been rewarding for him, as well. I treasure the times we have spent together.

Bruce may not realize that he is also my role model. At my request, he spoke to the Breakfast Club about being successful 16 years ago. His talk about integrity, honesty, and persistence in business struck a chord with me. At that time, I committed to be like him. I related to his background. We were both native Las Vegans. We were both were sports stars from Bishop Gorman High School. Sports brought us to UNLV and, basically, kept us going to college. We each had quit college at one time, and athletics brought us back. At Gorman High, we were exposed to very successful people and had

acquired a driving need to achieve success in a most honorable fashion. From that point forward, when Bruce spoke, I listened.

Our one minute conversation in an elevator inspired Amy and me to have our third child. His advice of about taking one of my children somewhere special every year led me to break my shoulder at Father/Son Fighter Pilots Camp. Ever since he suggested I sit on a non-profit board, I have continually served on various charities' Boards of Directors. I have also attempted to pass on some words of wisdom to a younger person struggling through life's challenges.

My life is immeasurably better since I met Bruce! My family and friends' lives are better as well, because I have become a much better person. He remains an inspiration to me daily.

Tito Tiberti

I guess I've known Bruce since the fifth grade, about as long as any of his friends. And looking back, I think he developed a survivor's instinct — early on. His parents divorced when we were teenagers. Later on he had to take his older brother Jimmy under his wing for a while, and that whole situation was uncomfortable, but he did a good job with it. Bruce showed a lot of character during those years. I remember he ate dinner at our house a lot, and he took a lot of odd jobs along the way. Finances were always a real issue for him, but he hung in there pretty well. Like a lot of us growing up, I don't think he had much career direction. But he was a good athlete, a good basketball and baseball player, and he learned a lot from sports about teamwork and staying competitive, which would serve him well in his career.

On the question of whether I knew Bruce would build the largest insurance business in the state, I can't say I would have predicted that, but I also wouldn't say that I'm really surprised by it. He's more driven than you might think, and he's a quick study. He's also a pretty good investor. He has an appreciation of money because it wasn't always there.

I had something to do with his getting initially diagnosed by Corey Brown. There had been a few signs that there was something going on there, and we finally pushed him to get an appointment. A doctor friend of ours, Jerry Sylvain, had actually noticed some symptoms in Bruce about a year before his diagnosis, in 1998, and Jerry called me after seeing us together at lunch and asked whether Bruce was all right. We had an incident where we were mugged on a trip to Sao Paolo about a year before and Bruce's wallet and credit cards were stolen, and that really seemed to put him out of sorts as well. It just seemed to have a huge impact on him mentally, and disoriented him more than it should have.

But, as is his nature, Bruce hasn't let this news dramatically affect his life. He's still trying to do as much as he can, and he's a great battler and a great friend. On a 1 to 10 scale, I'd say his attitude toward it is about an 8. He's not a blurry-eyed optimist that everything will be just fine, because he's too much of a realist; but he also will treat this battle with courage and intelligence. And like any great friend that you have been around all your life, he's just neat to be with, always reliable and always great fun.

Jim Williams

I met Bruce through our mutual friend Craig Sullivan, who spends his summers at Hayden Lake, Idaho, where we live. Craig arranged a phone call, and one day this guy calls and says, "So I hear that you're a Parkie." I'd never heard that expression to describe Parkinson's, but it made me laugh and we ended up chatting for about an hour.

I found Bruce to be instantly likable and a very caring person, and I liked his sense of humor. My hand will shake from time to time, and people will ask if I'm all right, and if it's a woman I'll say something like, "Better watch my hand. Don't get too close now." Once they see me joking about it, the nervousness goes away.

Bruce and I now talk maybe once a month and I always enjoy chatting with him. He's inspired me to help others with Parkinson's, and because of him I've probably met five or six other people who have it. I try to share information with them the same way he did with me.

I remember going to this one Parkinson's seminar in Spokane and all they talked about was the various medications that people were using to treat the disease. It was really a waste of time. Bruce understands the same thing I do: that the most important thing is to keep your body in shape, to get exercise, and to not just lie there and take medicine. I tell people, "So what if you're not in shape. Start today and get in shape. Life is not a dress rehearsal."

I'm 69 years old and I can bench press 275 pounds. I still fly fish, hunt, play tennis and golf and I lift weights regularly. I may die with Parkinson's disease because I'm not going to die from it. That's something Bruce and I have in common; we both have positive attitudes about this thing.

I also know that he's been very successful in his insurance business, but he doesn't make a big deal out of it. I've never been that impressed with money anyway. What impresses me is when I see that a person is a genuine and caring, and that describes Bruce. I'm really glad I got to know him.

Bill Wright

I've been working with Bruce since 1989 as a producer and salesman. We've been good friends all that time, as well as having an employer – employee relationship.

Our relationship has been good for both of us. I feel like I've been a good sounding board for him, sort of a moral compass at times, and he's helped me overcome a few character flaws. I've always been outspoken to a fault, and he's taught me the ability to bite my tongue on occasion, although my tendency is still to utter the awful truth.

Bruce's success is in part due to his talent for being a good administrator. He wants the best for his people. Oh, there are days when he's self-absorbed and oblivious, but there are also many days when he's very in tune with the people around him and empathetic to their problems and challenges.

Bruce has always been on a "personal betterment and improve the world" tour. We've gone on many corporate retreats, and he's always looking for ways to better the company and himself. He's been great about sharing information with others in the company, and has never felt threatened by those he works with. That can't be said about all bosses. He has also been very generous to those who do good work for him, unlike the current company bosses who are skinflints to a fault. They tend to be penny-wise and pound-foolish.

Bruce is also a good money manager, with a good sense of knowing when to spend money and when to conserve.

When Bruce first told me he was planning to run for Lieutenant Governor of Nevada, my first response was, "Are you crazy?" But his reasons were honorable. He said he felt it was a good time to give something back to the State. He was just halfway through his term on the Nevada Athletic Commission, so he had to resign that, but I think he was attracted by a new challenge and perhaps persuaded by people who convinced him he was well-known enough to have a chance. He would quickly learn that his name recognition outside of Las Vegas and his circle of friends was basically nil.

There were two things which really worked against Bruce in the campaign: 1) the fact that he was running as a Republican and yet was a close, lifelong friend of a Democratic governor; and 2) the state Republican Party never really got behind him. A $1,000 donation that he'd made to Bill Clinton in 1992, really at the behest of Bob Miller, became a major polarizing issue which got played up big time in the press.

Those two issues created a lot of mistrust for Bruce throughout the campaign, but I will say that he overcame a lot of that opposition because no one could work a room better than he could. He would go into a hostile environment, maybe a speaking engagement with 100 people, and he would shake every single hand in the room and engage everyone in conversation. It was just amazing how he could strip away people's opposition, and they would come away liking him. As I recall, Bruce made 140 appearances during the campaign and gave 110 speeches. He was tireless. I felt our internal campaign team did a better job than any of the outside advisors, but then that's just my opinion. We focused throughout on defeating John Mason, who we felt was just not a good candidate for a lot of reasons, and, while we might have been successful in doing that, we managed to help Lonnie Hammargren get elected. He had name recognition for always being in the newspaper for working on boxers with brain conditions and having a house that was like a junk yard museum. And it turns out that, because people knew his name, he got a lot more votes than we thought he would.

I will say it was a good thing for the company that Bruce didn't win. We all learned a lot from the experience, and it's easy to look back now and smile about it all. But make no mistake: we wanted to win and were disappointed when we didn't.

Like others, I sensed that something was wrong with Bruce about a year before he was diagnosed. I would say things like "Are you feeling okay?" or "You look like shit today!" I remember a symptom that turned out to be telling was that his handwriting kept getting smaller. He had what is called "micrographia," where there's a diminishment of the ability to move the hands and the penmanship gets tiny.

One day I came into his office and he was obviously depressed, and I said, "What's going on?" And he snapped back with, "I have Parkinson's, thank you very much."

I didn't know what to say, so I said something like, "It's probably just as well that you now know what it is, so that you can treat it properly."

I felt like he was in the dumps for about 60 to 90 days, but he's been extremely positive most of the time since then. I have a sense that he has a real fear of how bad it will get.

I think Bruce is a different guy since his diagnosis, but no better or worse. He's been a pleasure to work with and a good friend. You can't help but be inspired by a guy like that.

Epilogue
Moving Forward

Some might wonder where I'm going from here. You probably have already surmised that I'm not going to fade quietly into that good night. Rather, I'm going to wage a relentless battle in the next several years against Parkinson's disease, both for myself and for the hundreds of thousands of others in this country who are daily fighting this mysterious foe.

We need money, lots of it, to fund research to answer tough questions and to conduct far more laboratory experiments. And we need much more public education about the disease. It is estimated that there are tens of thousands of Parkinson's sufferers who are unaware what is causing them all the pain and confusion.

This book has been published for me, for my family and offspring, for my friends, and for my fellow "Parkies." All of the proceeds from its sale will go toward research to find the cure for our disease. But its message is for everyone: a positive attitude is essential, and courage is its own reward. The two add up to hope, and hope is everything. It keeps the glass full.

Bruce Layne